elines.

THE GREAT ENTERPRISE

ST. MARY'S COLLEGE   TRENCH HOUSE

This book is issued in accordance with current College
Library Regulations.

DATE DUE AT LIBRARY LAST STAMPED BELOW

The Armada Jewel.

THE GREAT ENTERPRISE

The History of the Spanish Armada

As revealed in contemporary
documents
selected and edited by
STEPHEN USHERWOOD

BELL & HYMAN
LONDON

Published in 1982 by
BELL & HYMAN LIMITED
Denmark House
37-39 Queen Elizabeth Street
London SE1 2QB

First published by The Folio Society, London

British Library Cataloguing in Publication Data
The Great enterprise.
1. Armada, 1588
I. Usherwood, Stephen
942.05′5   DA360

ISBN 0 7135 1309 8

PRINTED IN GREAT BRITAIN
Set in 12 pt Poliphilus, leaded 1 point

CONTENTS

ACKNOWLEDGEMENTS

The author wishes to acknowledge his wife Elizabeth's invaluable help at all stages of this book's preparation. He also thanks for their kind assistance Monsignor Charles Burns, Archivista dell'Archivio Segreto Vaticano; the Rector and students of the English College in Rome; the staff of the National Maritime Museum, Greenwich; and the librarians of the British Library, London.

ILLUSTRATIONS

ENDPAPERS

Introduction

The great enterprise that Philip II set in motion in 1586 led, two years later, to the first major battle in a long struggle. There had been hostilities on both sides of the Atlantic before this, but the Armada fight marked the beginning of a new kind of conflict, the first world war, in fact, since Philip ruled an empire on which the sun never set, and both sides employed a new weapon, the ocean-going galleon, armed with guns firing broadside.

This war had been preceded by a war of words, fought with another new weapon, the printing press. Protestant teaching, spreading from Germany and Switzerland, had led to terrible upheavals in France, the Netherlands, Scandinavia and the British Isles. Everywhere Protestants claimed to be restoring Christianity to a supposed pre-medieval purity, but the result was more like a revolution than a reformation. The Catholic church had suffered the dissolution of religious orders, the pulling down of innumerable buildings, the dispersal of priceless paintings and manuscripts and the mutilation of countless works of art, but, most serious of all, when this wave of destruction had passed, Catholics in many parts of northern Europe became subject to penal laws forbidding them to practise their religion.

Some years before Protestantism had taken deep root in England, Elizabeth's father, Henry VIII, had set aside his Spanish wife, Catherine of Aragon, and the reasons he gave for doing so made their daughter Mary appear illegitimate. Elizabeth was equally regarded as illegitimate by all those who held Mary to have been born in true wedlock. Thus what might otherwise have been a century of friendship between England and Spain ended in bitter strife. Even when Elizabeth, at the age of twenty-five, succeeded to the throne, it would still have been possible for Catholics and Protestants to live side by side in England and Ireland, but she decided otherwise. A Protestant Church was established and its forms of public worship became the only ones legally permitted. Catholics hoped that if Elizabeth died she would be succeeded on the throne by the Catholic Queen of Scots, Mary Stuart, who had been a prisoner in England since 1568, and that they would then be granted freedom of worship. After the execution of Mary on 8 February 1587 her twenty-year old son, James VI of Scotland, became next in line of succession, but he had been brought up a Protestant. As the danger of Spanish invasion came closer, the penal laws against Catholics were enforced with increasing severity.

In presenting these events in detail, the historian, unlike the writer of fiction, cannot give his readers a feeling of suspense. They know the tale's end before it begins, and can usually recall what happened, even if they do not remember the why and wherefore, but in place of suspense there is in what follows – letters and dispatches, proclamations and decrees, orders of battle and sailing instructions, many of them written in the heat of action – a sense of immediacy. As they wrote, king and queen, diplomat and sea captain, were unable to guess what the days ahead might bring, but today the reader, like the spectator at some drama of Euripides or Ibsen, can savour the irony behind the scripts, now brought out of those dusty chests and cupboards where faithful clerks once stored them, knowing them to be the very stuff of history. Here he is invited to see not only the conflict itself, but those deep and bitter causes for which fighting men on both sides, short of food, drink and ammunition, sought 'the bubble reputation even in the cannon's mouth' and, when the firing stopped, tasted the sweetness of victory or the sourness of defeat.

The reader may, nevertheless, say, like a playgoer late for the first act, that he cannot follow the plot because he does not understand what had happened before his arrival. In this book the drama begins in the year 1572 and the reader will quickly become aware that this was a troubled one for Elizabeth. In June she ordered the execution of the Catholic Earl of Northumberland and in July that of his accomplice in rebellion, the foremost nobleman in the kingdom, John Howard, fourth Duke of Norfolk. This was a delayed retribution for their attempted rescue of Mary, Queen of Scots, from her English prison. In August the Court went into mourning for the Protestants massacred in Paris on St Bartholomew's Day.

For Philip II, on the other hand, 1572 brought victory in the Mediterranean and mastery over its busy trade routes. The combined fleets of Spain and Italy annihilated the Turkish navy at Lepanto in the Gulf of Corinth. This may have led Philip to believe that his forces were invincible and certainly increased his admiration for the Marquis of Santa Cruz, one of the commanders on that great day. Nobody could ever, after this, drive home to Philip the lesson that Lepanto had been an old-style fight between equally matched fleets of galleys, not galleons.

By the 1580s young Englishmen from Catholic families, sent abroad to be educated for the priesthood at the English colleges in Douai, Valladolid and Rome, were returning on mission and, besides ministering to surviving Catholics, making many converts. Elizabeth's government was alarmed and enacted stringent laws against such priests and all who harboured them. The fear of a Catholic revival, and Anthony Babington's plot to rescue the Queen of Scots, at length brought Elizabeth to the point of signing Mary's death warrant. After her execution, Philip, whom his countrymen called the prudent king, hesitated no longer; he must liberate the English Catholics and at the same time clear the island of those pirates' nests from which so many raids had been made on Spanish ships and Spanish ports.

The sending of an invasion force direct from Spain, he had been told, would be an excessively expensive operation, especially when the upkeep of the Spanish army in the Netherlands was already causing the Duke of Parma, in spite of his victories over the Dutch, great anxiety. Philip, as an alternative to direct attack, insisted that Parma should provide the men and the sea transport for the invasion of Britain and that the Armada should escort them across the Channel.

When the Armada arrived off Plymouth, a running fight developed along the south coast. None of the captains on either side had any previous experience of operations involving so many sailing ships firing broadside against an enemy of equal strength and nautical skill. Drake had circumnavigated the world and Martin Frobisher had penetrated the waters of north-eastern Canada, but neither had ever sailed in so large a company under orders from a superior. Small wonder that Frobisher cursed Drake for leaving his watch in the middle of the night. The details to be found in the reports submitted by the opposing commanders leave little doubt why victory went to the English – they were within easy reach of home ports, had better weapons and faster ships, and were given one clear objective, to destroy the enemy by gunfire, avoiding boarders. The Spaniards were

at a disadvantage from the start; their men-of-war had, in effect, been
sent on convoy escort duty and were not free to bring on a general
engagement. Parma failed completely to perform what was required
of him. His army was not ready. At night, while the Armada lay in
an exposed position off Calais, the English sent fireships against it,
driving it from its anchorage. Next day the fleets met again off
Gravelines and English gunfire caused severe damage. Medina
Sidonia, fighting with conspicuous courage, ordered his ships to
retreat. A gale carried them in the direction of Scotland.

The English fleet, having exhausted its ammunition, followed for
some time, and then returned to port. For them England was indeed

> *This precious stone set in the silver sea,*
> *Which serves it in the office of a wall*
> *Or as a moat defensive to a house,*
> *Against the envy of less happier lands.*

For several weeks no one knew for certain where the great bulk of the
Armada was; it had in fact set course for Spain by way of the
Orkneys and the west coast of Ireland. About half of the ships that
had sailed in July reached home, but of their men fewer than a third
survived. Thirst, starvation and the cruel sea had carried off the
majority. On the Irish coast many ships put in for food and water,
and, caught by a violent hurricane, were battered to pieces on the
shore. Most of their crews were drowned, but over 1,000 got through
the surf, only to be stripped naked by the Irish and slaughtered by
armed bands of English soldiers. One Castilian, Captain Cuellar,
eventually escaped by way of Scotland to the Spanish Netherlands,
where, with everything fresh in his mind, he wrote the account of his
adventures with which this book ends.

In the documents that follow modern spelling has been used,
except in one or two cases. Most of the writers dictated the originals
to secretaries. Where they wrote in their own hand, a modern reader,
conditioned by standardized spelling, might conclude, erroneously,
that the writer was uncultured because his spelling was idiosyncratic.

It has been necessary to put a double date on some documents. In
1582 Continental countries accepted Pope Gregory XIII's revision
of the Julian (Old Style) calendar, which at that time was 10 days in
arrear – for example, an English source will state that fighting with
the Armada began on 20 July, but the Spaniards call it 30 July, and

where it appears at the head of Spanish documents it is printed 20/30 July.

Chapters are arranged in pairs; documents emanating from England and her friends take first place, and those from Spain and other sources the second. It is thus possible to view the same event through the eyes of the men who actually opposed each other at the council table or in battle. Non-combatants tend to believe every rumour that fits in with their preconceptions, whereas soldiers and sailors remain objective, never pretending that defeat is not disaster; if victorious, they rejoice; if vanquished, they accept their fate with dignity.

CHAPTER ONE

War of Words: The Scottish Pawn

What, the sword and the word? do you
study them both, master parson?
                    Merry Wives of Windsor III i 38

Before a medieval fight it commonly occurred that heralds crossed the no man's
land between the opposing armies with messages of defiance, calls to parley or
offers of peace. So too in this conflict, when the Armada arrived off Plymouth
the Lord High Admiral 'sent his pinnace, the Dolphin, to give the Duke of
Medina defiance', but, for many years before that, a war of words had been
carried on all over Europe. In Britain it was but human to see the protagonists
either in black or white: Mary Queen of Scots, to her enemies, an adulteress
and an accomplice in the murder of her husband, the father of her only child;
to her friends, the beautiful victim of forged letters and treacherous rebellion;
and Elizabeth of England, to her friends the Virgin Queen, the saviour of
religion; to her foes, the illegitimate daughter of a tyrant who had usurped the
functions of the Papacy.

Mary took refuge in England in 1568, imagining that she would be given
assistance for the recovery of the Scottish throne. Elizabeth, who had
previously professed friendship, kept her under strict surveillance for the next
eighteen years. The two queens never met. In captivity Mary seemed a mere
pawn on the chessboard of international politics, but in a period when assassina-
tion, rebellion and massacre were commonplace, it was always possible that the
day would come when she would be proclaimed Queen of England. By her
twenty-seventh year grief for her first husband, the horrible jealousy of
Darnley, the ruthless ambition of Bothwell, had become only torturing
memories, yet even her gaolers admitted the fascination of a spirit unquenched
by circumstances that would have driven most men mad. That a priest of the
Church of England, whom Elizabeth made in succession Bishop of Worcester,
Bishop of London and Archbishop of York, should be moved by Mary's
condition not to pity, but murderous enmity, is a measure of the extent and
ferocity of the conflict.

Walsingham's letter to Critoy, a friend in Paris, is another example of how words can be manipulated to make black appear white. After the revolt of the Earls of Westmorland and Northumberland in 1569 over 800 peasants were hanged in the northern counties, yet Walsingham can write: 'her [the Queen's] proceedings towards the papists was with great lenity.'

Similarly an Anglican chaplain, addressing Catholic prisoners in the Tower, shows by the violence of his language that, for him, no member of the Society of Jesus can be a Christian.

From Edwin Sandys, Bishop of London, to William Cecil, Lord Burghley, 1572

1 Forthwith to cut off the Scottish queen's head.
2 To remove from our queen papists and such as by private persua-sion overthrow good counsel.
3 The queen's majesty to be guarded strongly with Protestants; and others to be removed.
4 Order must be taken for the safe keeping of the Tower, and for good order to be had in London for strengthening of the city, and that they receive no papist of strength to sojourn there this winter.
5 A firm league to be made with the young Scottish king and the Protestants there.
6 A league to be made with the princes Protestant of Germany, offensive and defensive.
7 The chief papists of this realm are to be shut up in the Tower, and the popish old bishops to be returned thither.
8 The Gospel earnestly to be promoted, and the church not burdened with unnecessary ceremonies.
9 The Protestants, which only are faithful subjects, are to be com-forted, preferred and placed in authority; the papists are to be displaced.

These put in execution, would turn to God's glory, the safety of the queen's majesty and make the realm flourish and stand.

Burghley, at this time forty-eight, was regarded throughout Europe as an incomparable counsellor. Queen Elizabeth called him her 'spirit', and em-ployed him on all important affairs of state for the first forty years of her reign, though she did not always take his advice. When he lay dying, she came to his bedside and fed him with her own hand.

From Sir Francis Walsingham, to Monsieur Critoy, 1581

. . . Her Majesty, at her coming to the crown, utterly disliking the
tyranny of Rome, which had used by terror and rigour to settle
commandments of men's faiths and consciences; though as a princess
of great wisdom and magnanimity she suffered but the exercise of one
religion; yet her proceedings towards the papists was with great
lenity . . . But when, about the twentieth year of her reign, she had
discovered in the King of Spain an intention to invade her dominions;
and that a principal part of the plot was, to prepare a party within the
realm, that might adhere to the foreigner; and that the seminaries
began to blossom and to send forth daily priests and professed men,
who should by vow taken at shrift reconcile her subjects from their
obedience, yea, and bind many of them to attempts against her
Majesty's sacred person; and that, by the poison which they spread,
the humours of most papists were altered, and that they were no more
papists in conscience, and of softness, but papists in faction; then
were there new laws made for the punishment of such as should
submit themselves to such reconcilements, or renunciation of obedience. And because it was a treason carried in the clouds, and in
wonderful secrecy, and come seldom to light; and that there was no
presuspicion thereof so great as the recusancy to come to divine
service, because it was set down by their decrees, that to come to
church after reconcilement was absolutely heretical and damnable.
Therefore there were added laws containing punishment pecuni-
ary . . .

The other party, which have been offensive to the state though in
another degree, which named themselves *reformers*, and we commonly call *puritans*, this hath been the proceeding towards them; a
great while, when they inveighed against such abuses in the church
as pluralities, nonresidence, and the like, their zeal was not condemned, only their violence was sometimes censured. When they
refused the use of some ceremonies and rites, as superstitious, they were
tolerated with much connivance and gentleness; yea, when they
called in question the superiority of bishops, and pretended to a
democracy into the church, yet their propositions were here considered, and by contrary writings debated and discussed. Yet all this
while it was perceived that their course was dangerous, and very
popular; as, because papistry was odious, therefore it was ever in

their mouths, that they sought to purge the church from the relics of papistry; a thing acceptable to the people, who love ever to run from one extreme to another.

But now of late years, when they began both to vaunt of their strength, and number of their artisans and followers, and to use commination that their cause would prevail through uproar and violence; then it appeared to be no more zeal, no more conscience, but mere faction and division; and therefore, though the state were compelled to hold somewhat a harder hand to restrain them than before, yet was it with as great moderation as the peace of the state or church could permit . . .

Walsingham

Sir Francis Walsingham was, after Burghley, the most powerful man in the Privy Council. M. Critoy was a friend whom he had made when ambassador in Paris.

Minute of the Privy Council, 23 September 1586

Fourteen of the late conspirators were executed on the 20 and 21 of this month, mostly gentlemen of good houses.

Thomas Wilkes, Secretary of the Privy Council

The conspirators were Catholics of good family who, led by Anthony Babington, had become involved in a plot, detected by Walsingham's agents, to assassinate Elizabeth and place Mary, Queen of Scots, on the throne. They were hung, drawn and quartered at Tyburn. Evidence of Mary's complicity had also been obtained.

From the Lords and Commons, to Elizabeth I, November 1586

May it please your most excellent majesty, we, your humble, loving and faithful subjects, the lords and commons in this present parliament assembled, having of longtime to our intolerable grief, seen by how manifold, most dangerous and execrable practices, Mary, commonly called the Queen of Scots, hath compassed the destruction of your majesty's sacred and most royal person and thereby not only to bereave us of the sincere and true religion of Almighty God, bringing us and this noble crown back again into the thraldom of the Romish tyranny, but also utterly to ruinate and overthrow the happy state and commonweal of this realm, . . . do most humbly beseech . . .

The Armada Portrait of Queen Elizabeth I, attributed to George Gower.

Mary, Queen of Scots, and her son James VI and I in 1583.

Arrangements for the execution of Mary, Queen of Scots, at
Fotheringhay Castle. This contemporary sketch simultaneously
depicts the Queen's entry, preparation and execution.

that direction be given for further proceedings against the said Scottish queen, according to the effect and true meaning of the said statute: . . . we cannot find that there is any possible means to provide for your majesty's safety, but by the just and speedy execution of the said queen . . .

The Lords and Commons

From Elizabeth I, to the Lords and Commons

That her highness, moved with some commiseration for the Scottish queen, in respect of her former dignity and great fortunes in her younger years, her nearness of kindred to her majesty and also of her sex, could be well pleased to forbear the taking of her blood, if by any other means to be devised by her highness's Great Council of this realm, the safety of her majesty's person and government might be preserved, without danger of ruin and destruction, and else not; therein leaving them all nevertheless to their own free liberty and dispositions of proceeding otherwise at their choice.

The Queen

From the Lords and Commons, to Elizabeth I

That having often conferred and debated on that question, according to her highness's commandment, they could find no other way than was set down in their petition.

The Lords and Commons

From Elizabeth I, to the Lords and Commons

If I should say unto you that I mean not to grant your petition, by my faith I should say unto you more than perhaps I mean. And if I should say unto you I mean to grant your petition, I should then tell you more than is fit for you to know. And thus I must deliver you an answer answerless.

The Queen

From Thomas Wilkes, special envoy in the Netherlands, to Sir Francis Walsingham, 14 December 1586

I hold it [the execution of Mary Queen of Scots] fitter to be done than not done. If I might receive some abstract of her crimes and the manner of proceeding held against her I should hold myself greatly bound to you, and I suppose it would do good here to satisfy many men that hold the course taken against her somewhat strange, considering her quality.

The Hague,

Thomas Wilkes

From Elizabeth I, to you at our Castle of Fotheringhay, February 1587

Divers Things were compassed and imagined within this Realm of England by Anthony Babington and others with the Privity of the said Mary, pretending to the Crown of this Realm of England, tending to the Hurt, Death and Destruction of our Royal Person. At the humble Petition and instant Suit of the Lords and Commons in this present Parliament assembled we, deeply foreseeing the continual dangers that we and this whole Realm do stand in through the said dangerous Practices, and seeing withal that by the ancient Laws of this our Realm they do justly deserve Death, and that all the Favours and Tolerance by us heretofore used towards the said Mary have, and do, embolden her and her Confederates to persevere in their mischievous Attempts against us and this our Realm, do hereby direct and command you that at our Castle of Fotheringhay in our County of Northampton you do immediately cause the head of the same Mary to be cut off; whereof fail ye not.

The Queen

On 8 February Mary met her end with great dignity, firmly asserting her Catholic faith. When the news reached London bonfires were lit amid great rejoicings, but the Queen displayed terrible anger and grief, declaring that Burghley had sent the warrant without consulting her.

From Father John Feckenham, former Abbot of Westminster, to the Privy Council, 1570

I desire, I say, to make my humble suit to your worships for myself and my prison fellows both, that hereafter we may not be haled up by the arms to the church in such violent manner against our wills, against all former example, against the doctrine of your own side, (Luther, Bucer, Bullinger, Zwingli, Œcolampadius, Melanchthon, and the rest, every one writing and earnestly persuading that all violence be taken away in matters of religion,) there to hear such preachers as care not what they say, so they somewhat say against the professed faith of Christ's catholic church. And there to hear a sermon, not of persuading us, but of railing upon us. This, if your worships will incline unto for charity's sake, we shall have to render you most humble thanks, and whatsoever else we may do in this our heavy time of imprisonment.

Tower of London,

Father John Feckenham

A book by Œcolampadius, once owned by Henry VIII and Catherine of Aragon, and bearing their arms on its leather binding, is now in the Chained Library of Hereford Cathedral.

CHAPTER TWO

War of Words: The Catholic Cause

Essos reyes poderosos
que vemos por escrituras
ya passadas,
con casos triestes llorosos
ueron sus buenas venturas
trastornàdas;
assí que no hay cosa fuerte,
y perlados
assí los trata la Muerte
que a papas y emperadores
como a los pobres pastores
de ganados.

Coplas por la muerte de su padre
JORGE MANRIQUE. (1440–1479)

(Those mighty kings that we see in the writings of long ago, by sad and lamentable events catastrophe overtook their good fortunes. So nothing is sure, for popes, emperors and prelates are treated by Death even as poor cowherds.)

There is a passage in the letter transcribed below from the Queen of Scots to Pope Pius V so worded that she unconsciously reveals one of the tests by which both sides in the controversy between Catholic and Protestant decided where a person stood. She admits that an English minister, sent to her by her guards, had offered in her presence 'certain prayers in the vulgar tongue', i.e. English, and that, because she had listened, a report had been put out (which she begs Pius not to believe) that she had changed her religion. Preposterous as this may sound four hundred years later, it was then regarded as a clear defeat for the Catholic cause if a Catholic could be persuaded, or forced, to worship 'in the vulgar tongue', and for him to receive Holy Communion according to the Anglican rite prescribed by Elizabeth was regarded, both by Protestants and by Catholics, as a sign of apostasy. It was in such an atmosphere that Catholics, in order to attend Mass in Latin, risked torture and death and the priests that served them were so often sentenced to be hung, drawn and quartered.

The Pope during whose reign the Armada was launched, Sixtus V, regarded the rebuilding of a ruinous part of Rome as his major concern. His fiery and energetic nature could scarcely endure Philip II's slow caution. He wished to see the kingdom of England recovered for the Church without delay, before Elizabeth and her men of war, whose prowess he admired, had time to prepare, and so he offered Philip II 1,000,000 gold crowns on condition that Parma's army actually landed in England. As the Armada failed, he paid nothing.

From Mary, Queen of Scots, to Pope Pius V, 30 November 1568

I, having been advertised that it hath been related unto the King of Spain, my lord and good brother, that I am become variable in the Catholic religion, although I have within some days past written to your Holiness devoutly to kiss your feet, and recommending me unto you, I do now again most humbly beseech you to hold me for a most devout and a most obedient daughter of the holy Catholic Roman church, and not to give faith unto those reports which may easily come, or shall hereafter come to your ears, that I have changed my religion, thereby to deprive me of your Holiness' grace and the favour of other Catholic princes. The same hath touched my heart so much, that I could not fail to write again of now to your Holiness, to complain and bemoan myself of the wrongs and of the injuries which they do unto me. I beseech the devout Christian princes and obedient sons of your Holiness, exhorting them to interpose their credit and authority which they have with the Queen of England, in whose power I am, to obtain of her that she will let me go out of her country, whither I came, secured by her promises, to demand aid of her against my rebels; and if nevertheless she will retain me, by all means yet that she will permit me to exercise my religion, which hath been forbidden to me, for which I am grieved and vexed in this kingdom. They so wrought that an English minister was sometimes brought to the place where I am straitly kept, which was wont to say certain prayers in the vulgar tongue; and because I am not at my own liberty, nor permitted to use any other religion, I have not refused to hear him, thinking I had committed no error. Wherein nevertheless, most holy father, if I have offended or failed in that or any thing else, I ask *misericordia* of your Holiness, beseeching the same to pardon and to absolve me, and to be sure and certain that I have never had any other will than constantly to live the most devout and most obedient daughter of the holy Catholic Roman church, in which I will live and die according to your Holiness' advices and precepts. I offer to make such amends and penance that all Catholic princes, especially your Holiness as monarch of the world, shall have occasion to rest satisfied and contented with me.

Written from Castle Bolton, the last of November, 1568.

The most devout and obedient

Daughter of your Holiness,

The Queen of Scotland, Widow of France,

Maria.

Mary, who is writing from Yorkshire soon after her arrival in England, signs herself 'Widow of France', recalling her first husband Francis II, who died when she was eighteen. Her second husband, Henry Stuart, Lord Darnley, had been murdered. The Earl of Bothwell, her third husband, whom she had married according to the Protestant rite, was a refugee in Denmark.

From Pope Pius V, to The World, 1569

A declaratory sentence of our holy lord Pope Pius V against Elizabeth, pretender Queen of England, and all heretics adhering to her. By virtue of which sentence all her subjects are absolved from their oath of allegiance, and all other engagements whatsoever; and those who for the future shall obey her are pronounced excommuni-cated...

Pius V

For the first four years of his reign Pius V had heard many reports of the persecution of Catholics in England. No pope could have remained silent, but Pius, by his tactlessness, put all English Catholics in danger of being regarded as traitors. This 'sentence' was not a 'Bull', though often called so.

From *History of Martyrdom of 12 priests* by Dr William Allen

This virtuous Priest, M. Nelson, was taken in London upon 1 December 1577, late in the evening, as he was saying the Nocturne of the Matins for the next day following, and was presently sent to prison upon suspicion of Papistry, as they term the Catholic faith.

And after five or six days he was brought forth to be examined before the High Commissioners, and there they tendered the oath of the Queen's supremacy unto him, the which he refused to take. Being asked why he would not swear, he answered because he never had heard or read that any lay Prince could have that pre-eminence. Being farther demanded, who then was the head of the Church, he answered sincerely and boldly, that the Pope's Holiness was, to whom that supreme authority was due, as being Christ's vicar and the lawful successor of St Peter.

Secondly they asked him his opinion of the religion now practised in England, to which he answered promptly that it was both schismatical and heretical. Whereupon they bid him define what schism was, he told them that it was a voluntary departure from the unity of the Catholic Roman faith.

Then they inferred, 'What, is the Queen a schismatic, or no?' He answered, he could not tell, because he knew not her mind in setting forth or maintaining the religion now publicly used in England. Then the Commissioners replied that the Queen did promulgate it and maintain it; and urging him that if she so did, then whether she was a schismatic and heretic or no?

M. Nelson paused a while, as being loth to exasperate his prince, if he might have chosen [otherwise], but yet more loth to offend God and his own conscience or to give scandal to the world, answered conditionally after this sort: 'If she be the setter forth and defender of this religion now practised in England, then she is a Schismatic and an Heretic.' Which answer when they had wrung from him, they said he had spoken enough, they sought for no more at his hands.

When he was brought forth of the prison [14 February 1578], and to be laide on the hurdle, some of the officers exhorted him to ask the Queen's Majesty, whom he had highly offended, forgiveness, he answered, 'I will ask her no pardon, for because I never offended her.' At which words the people that stood about him raged, and threatened him that if he would not he should be hanged like a traitor as he was, 'Well', said he, 'God's will be done. I perceive that I must die, and surely I am ready to die with a good will. For better it is to abide all punishment, be it never so grievous here, than to suffer the eternal torments of hell fire.'

Dr Allen, a former principal of St Mary Hall, Oxford, was one of several distinguished scholars, who, finding the only two English universities, Oxford and Cambridge, closed to Catholics, went abroad to work. It was impossible to obtain a Catholic education in England, so he set up English colleges on the Continent. The students had few books and no amenities, but great enthusiasm; many entered the priesthood and volunteered to return to England on mission, knowing that they were going to almost certain death.

From Mary, Queen of Scots, to Bernardino de Mendoza in Paris,
20 May 1586

Considering the great obstinacy of my son in his heresy, for which, I can assure you, I weep and lament day and night, more even than for my own calamity, and foreseeing how difficult it will be for the Catholic church to triumph if he succeeds to the throne of England, I have resolved that, in case my son should not submit before my death to the Catholic religion (of which I may say that I see but small hope, whilst he remains in Scotland), I will cede and make over, by will, to the King your master, my right to the succession to this [English] crown, and beg him consequently to take me in future entirely under his protection, and also the affairs of this country. For the discharge of my own conscience, I could not hope to place them in the hands of a prince more zealous in our Catholic faith, or more capable, in all respects of re-establishing it in this country, as the interests of all Christendom demand. I am obliged in this matter to consider the public welfare of the Church before the private aggrandisement of my posterity. I again beg you most urgently that this should be kept secret, as if it becomes known it will cause the loss of my dowry in France, and bring about an entire breech with my son in Scotland, and my total ruin and destruction in England.
    Chartley, England,

Maria

Bernardino de Mendoza, Spanish Ambassador in Paris, was old, credulous, and fond of intrigue. Earlier Elizabeth had asked for his removal from the London embassy in view of his complicity in a plot against her. Mary had been moved to Chartley manor, Derbyshire, from Tutbury castle in the well-founded hope that a taste of freedom might tempt her to listen to agents provocateurs and become involved in Babington's plot.

From Giovanni Dolfin, Venetian Ambassador in Paris, to the Doge & Senate, 23 December 1586/2 January 1587

... [The French envoy, M. de Bellièvre] reports that he has had an interview with Her Majesty, and in obedience to his orders, he used every possible means to obtain the release of the Queen of Scotland. Her Majesty replied that she was greatly surprised to find that the King [of France], who on so many occasions had proved his affection for her begotten by her natural regard for him, should now endeavour, by a special embassy, by such vehement insistence, by employing so trusted a servant, to save the life of one who had so iniquitously compassed hers. Bellièvre left Her Majesty unshaken in her resolve by the many powerful arguments in favour of the Queen of Scotland; and the sentence was published condemning the Queen to death. The population of London wished to show their great contentment at this resolve by fireworks all over the city at night.

The sentence was read to the Queen of Scotland; by it she was deprived of the title of Queen, of the insignia of royalty and of her servants, and condemned to death. The Queen of England's officers began at once to give effect to this sentence. A Minister of the Church went to the Queen of Scotland to do his business with many perverse arguments to which the Queen replied as follows: that Catholic she had lived and Catholic she would die; from the Roman, the only true Church, she had instilled into her heart the holy faith, for which she would expose her blood and her life to a thousand deaths and a thousand torments; that she marvelled at the presumption with which he ventured to execute his orders.

M. de Bellièvre went once more to the Queen of England, to whom he made great complaint both of the sentence and the mode in which it was passed; he declared that, owing to its unwonted nature it had greatly disturbed the King [of France], who could not fail to feel deeply hurt by such treatment of the Queen of Scotland, so closely allied to him by blood and by affection.

Dolfin

The Doge and Senate needed to have the best intelligence service in the world, since the merchants of the republic lent money all over Europe and the Levant. Portugal, annexed by Philip II in 1580, had granted them special facilities as far away as Ormuz at the mouth of the Persian Gulf.

From Hieronimo Lippomano, Venetian Ambassador in Madrid, to the Doge & Senate, 2/12 January 1587

Don Juan d'Idiaquez came today to visit me, which he said he did also in the King's name. Don Juan talked of many subjects, among others he said that the Queen of England made a poor return to his Catholic Majesty for having freed her from prison. The King was resolved to keep up a large fleet to clear the ocean of pirates, and one day or other the Queen would receive her punishment, which would be all the severer the longer it was delayed. As these words were used by a Minister of such importance who may be said to do everything, they were as though spoken by the voice of the King, and so I have not hesitated to report them to your Serene Highness. It is indeed a miracle to see how he governs this great machine without any Council of State, and almost, one might say, without Ministers. But his long experience, and his singular prudence, joined to his great power, easily point out to him along sound and excellent lines of action more easily than they could occur to many, however wise they might be. All the same, considering his Majesty's age, we must hold that he will not be able to support these long fatigues entailed on him by his desire to examine and to know every detail; and as his son is so young he will be forced soon to elect Ministers of experience so that after his death a young Prince and inexperienced Ministers may not be left to the government of so many Kingdoms and States.

Lippomano

Lippomano, though on friendly terms with Don Juan d'Idiaquez, a principal secretary of state, underestimated the will-power of the ageing king, who continued faithfully to follow the advice of his father, the Emperor Charles V, 'Do everything yourself'.

From Philip II, to the Marqués de Olivares, Spanish Ambassador in Rome, 1/11 February 1587

You will cautiously approach his Holiness [Pope Sixtus V, elected 1585], and in such terms as you think fit endeavour to obtain from him a second brief declaring that, failing the Queen of Scotland, the right to the English crown falls to me. My claim, as you are aware, rests upon my descent from the House of Lancaster, and upon the will made by the Queen of Scotland, and mentioned in a letter from her, of which the copy is enclosed herewith. You will impress upon his Holiness that I cannot undertake a war in England for the purpose merely of placing upon that throne a young heretic like the King of Scotland who, indeed, is by his heresy incapacitated to succeed. His Holiness must, however, be assured that I have no intention of adding England to my own dominions, but to settle the crown upon my daughter the Infanta.

Madrid,

The King

Two hundred years earlier Catherine, daughter of John of Gaunt, Duke of Lancaster, and sister of Henry IV of England, married Philip's ancestor Henry of Castile. The second of Gaunt's three wives was Constance of Castile.

From Philip II, to Bernadino de Mendoza, in Paris, 21/31 March 1587

I have been deeply hurt by the death of the Queen of Scotland, of which I learn by yours of 28 February. It is very fine for the Queen of England now to want to give out that it was done without her wish, the contrary being so clearly the case. It will be well to convey to the Scots ambassador my sorrow at the event, and that I would send to condole with his King, and again offer him my friendship and the goodwill I always bore to his mother, only that I wish to avoid arous-ing suspicions which might harm him with his enemies.

San Lorenzo, [the Palace-Monastery known as the Escorial],

The King

From the Marqués de Olivares, to Philip II, 20/30 June 1587

On the 26th his Holiness was in a great rage at table, railing at those who served him and throwing the crockery about furiously, which he is rather in the habit of doing, but not often so violently as this.

It was noticed that this immediately followed an audience he had given to the French ambassador, who had received a despatch from his king on the previous day and sent an answer on the morrow. I had audience the day following, and although I found his Holiness otherwise favourable he said amongst other things that he was much alarmed at the jealousy that the King of France had begun to entertain of the House of Guise, and hoped it would lead him into no absurdity.

Rome,

Olivares

Pope Sixtus V's alarm was justified. On 23 December 1588 Henry III lured the Duke of Guise into the royal bedchamber at the Chateau of Blois and had him stabbed to death.

From Philip II, to the Marqués de Olivares, 14/24 June 1587

It will be advisable not to press forward for the present the question of the succession, but only in due time to request the Pope to fulfil the document of 24 February 1586, in which he undertook to accept the deprivation of the King of Scotland and to conform to my opinion with regard to the succession. On the other point, of declaring this war a righteous one, although it will be advisable for the reasons you and Allen have drawn up, yet it would be well for his Holiness at the time of the execution to grant a jubilee for those who take part in it, and those who pray for the success of so just and holy a cause . . .

It is also very desirable that you should now ensure the payment of the million, and its anticipation in the form I wrote on the 7 April. This should be done with all possible speed and certainty, without pledging me to any fixed time, although you should say that you are sure I shall carry out the enterprise as soon as I can out of regard to the service of the Lord, the obligations imposed upon us all by the death of the Queen of Scotland, and the saintly wishes of his Holiness. This is the path you will follow, but get the question of the money settled at once and let me know.

With regard to the hat for Allen; you will ask his Holiness from me to confer it at once, on the ground that, now that the Queen of Scotland, the hope of the English Catholics, is gone, they may despair, unless they see some person to whom they can turn for a remedy in their troubles. This danger may be avoided if they have a countryman of their own in high station near the person of the Pope, and particularly a person whom they know and trust so much as Allen. This will be a good public reason; but in addition, you will privately tell his Holiness that in the interests of the enterprise it is necessary to come to some understanding with certain persons in

England, and it is quite time, indeed more than time, that such preparations were commenced by the elevation in question. This will reinforce the other reasons you will urge, but all appearance that the elevation is made on account of the enterprise must be avoided.

The King

The king was wholly misinformed. The idea that English Catholics would welcome the invading forces as liberators was absurd. The instalment of Dr William Allen as Cardinal Archbishop in Canterbury would not have altered this.

From Bernardino de Mendoza, to Philip II, 16/26 June 1588

The resident English ambassador here has sent secretly to the Duke of Guise, offering him on behalf of his mistress assistance in money against this king. Guise replied that, so far from wishing for any help from her, he would employ all the strength he possessed until he saw her ruined and hanged; and if a hangman could not be found, he himself would willingly put the rope round her neck. He requested that she would send him no more such messages, for if she did he would throw out of the window the man who brought them, and would never admit within his doors any man attached to the embassy.

Considering the cunning devices they use here, it may be concluded they arranged for Guise to be tempted in this way, in order to discover whether he was so firm as he is; and if they found he was not, they would have accused him of accepting the aid of the Queen of England whilst he was insisting upon this king's withdrawing from his alliance with her.

Paris,

Mendoza

CHAPTER THREE

Cold War: Provocation and Prevarication

Words to the heat of deeds too cold breath gives.
                                                    Macbeth II i 58

The discovery by the Spaniards of the Potosi silver mines in Peru in 1545 and the establishment of an imperial mint there stimulated commerce of every kind both in the Americas and in Europe. Piracy along the new shipping routes, an irresistible temptation to many for whom honest trading was too slow a method of making a fortune, particularly appealed to the English and Dutch. Burghley, with characteristic foresight, strongly disapproved of piracy on the ground that covert hostilities could lead to open war. The Queen on the other hand was prepared to take risks and invested in the private adventures of Drake, the Earl of Cumberland and others; if they came home laden with 'purchase', as it was euphemistically called, they were welcome. In 1585 numerous English and Dutch ships, cargoes and crews peacefully engaged in traditional trade with Spain were seized on orders from Philip II while they lay in harbour at Bilbao and other Biscay ports. Parliament took great offence, but the King knew that the same London merchants whose ships he had taken also owned privateers operating against Spanish and Portuguese traders on the high seas. As a reprisal Drake, having assembled thirty armed London merchantmen and 2,000 soldiers, set out for the Caribbean. On the way they did great damage in the Canaries and Cape Verde Islands. At San Domingo, Hispaniola, the finest and largest of the new Spanish-built towns in the West Indies, Drake extorted a ransom of 25,000 ducats. His raid on Cadiz in 1587 was successful in delaying the departure of the Armada for a year, during which the queen carried on insincere peace negotiations with Parma, and attempted to ensure that the French would not give aid and comfort to Philip II's forces.

Homily by John Keltridge, preacher, to the Jesuits imprisoned in the Tower of London, 1581

Convince me, then, and condemn me. Is it because your religion cometh of sin? Then be ashamed; profess God's word. Is it because all your trumpery proceedeth of the pope? Revolt, return, amend, and deny him; stay upon the Lord God. Is it because the inventors of your mass have been such as was also your service invented? Filthy, ungodly, wicked, devilish, evil-disposed, naughty persons, and idolaters? Why you may forsake them when you will. But is it because that I open you the truth, because I tell you of the sins of your fathers and your own? because I tell you of your manifold ly-ings, great untruths, slanderous reproaches, filthy demeanour, un-godly life, evil deeds, erroneous opinions, foolish ceremonies, popish decrees, and whorish fables, which you have brought in and would confirm in England? I exhort you then in the name of the Lord to eschew and abhor them all. You that be here, coming from the pope, how can you stand so boldly, and face it out so gazingly, and hear us so repiningly, and spurn so irksomely as you do, without horror of conscience? We cannot suffer you, we may not suffer you, to defend so horrible and erroneous constitutions as your forefathers, the wicked popes, invented.

From Sir Thomas Tresham, to Elizabeth I, 1584

Let not us, your Catholic native English and obedient subjects, stand in more peril for frequenting the Blessed Sacrament and exercising the Catholic religion (and that most secretly) than do the Catholic subjects to the Turk publicly.

Thomas Tresham

Sir Thomas was a wealthy Northamptonshire landowner who, being a Catholic, refused to attend Anglican church services on Sundays and feast days as all citizens were required to do by the 1559 Act of Uniformity. For this recusancy, as it was called, he cheerfully paid repeated and heavy fines, and in addition, on the approach of the Armada was placed in custody by the Bishop of Ely. Many other Catholic recusants were similarly treated.

An Act against Jesuits, seminary priests and such other like dis-obedient persons, 1585

Whereas divers persons called or professed Jesuits, seminary priests and other priests, which have been and from time to time are made

in the parts beyond the seas by or according to the order and rites of
the Romish Church, have of late years come and been sent, and daily
do come and are sent, into this realm of England and other the
Queen's Majesty's dominions, of purpose (so hath appeared as well
by sundry means and proofs) not only to withdraw her Highness'
subjects from their due obedience to her Majesty but also to stir up
and move sedition, rebellion and open hostility within her Highness'
realms and dominions, to the great dangering of the safety of her
most royal person and to the utter ruin, desolation and overthrow of
the whole realm. For reformation whereof be it ordained, established
and enacted by the Queen's most excellent Majesty and the Lords
spiritual and temporal and the Commons in Parliament, that all and
every Jesuits, seminary priests and other priests whatsoever, made or
ordained out of the realm of England or other her Highness' dominions or within any of her Majesty's realms or dominions by any
authority, power or jurisdiction derived, challenged or pretended
from the see of Rome since the feast of the Nativity of St John
Baptist in the first year of her Highness' reign, shall within forty days
next after the end of this present session of Parliament depart out of
this realm of England and out of all other her Highness' realms and
dominions, if the wind, weather and passage shall serve for the same;
or else so soon after the end of the said forty days as the wind weather
and passage shall so serve.

   And be it further enacted by the authority that it shall not be lawful to or for any Jesuit, seminary priest or other such priest, deacon or
any religious or ecclesiastical person whatsoever, being born within
this realm or any other her Highness' dominions, to come into, be or
remain in any part of this realm or any other her Highness' dominions
after the end of the same forty days, and if he do, that then every such
offence shall be taken and adjudged to be high treason. And every
person which shall wittingly and willingly receive, relieve, comfort,
aid or maintain any such Jesuit etc., shall also for such offence be
adjudged a felon without benefit of clergy, and suffer death, loss and
forfeit as in case of one attainted of felony.

                                                              Elizabeth

*Five years before this Act was passed, Father Edmund Campion, a former
Oxford scholar who entered the Jesuit order while studying abroad, had returned on mission and made many converts. These were known as 'reconciled'*

Sir Francis Walsingham, *c.* 1530–1590.

Sir Christopher Hatton, 1540–1591.

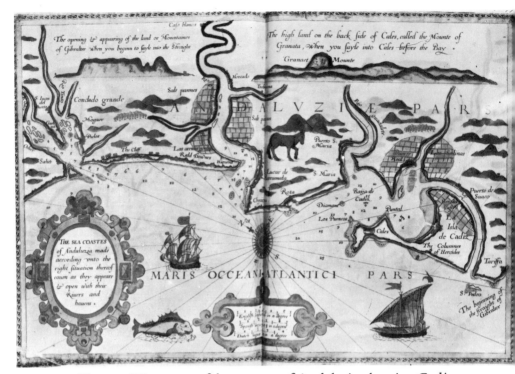

Chart, or Waggoner, of the sea coast of Andalusia, showing Cadiz.
From *The Mariner's Mirrour* published in 1588.

The Ark Royal.

Catholics, and were considered by the government much more dangerous than 'old' Catholics. Campion was caught in 1580, accused of conspiring against the queen's life, and tortured in the Tower. At his trial the Privy Council offered no evidence of a plot, but he was hung, drawn and quartered at Tyburn together with Fathers Ralph Sherwin and Alexander Briant.

Under the Act persecution of Catholics became much fiercer. Margaret Clitherow, the convert wife of a Protestant butcher in York, was charged with harbouring priests, though the only evidence offered was the finding of Mass vestments in her house. She was pressed to death in the Toll Booth prison on Ousebridge, York, on 25 March 1586.

Sir Thomas Tresham was one of those reconciled, probably by Campion. His correspondence was found in 1605 walled up in his beautiful mansion at Rushton.

From John Hawkins, Treasurer of the Navy, to William Cecil, Lord Burghley, 28 December 1585

A note to show the commodity that would grow to her Majesty and country by increasing the wages of the servitors by sea in her High-ness' ships. By this mean her Majesty's ships will be furnished with able men, such as can make shift for themselves, keep themselves clean without vermin and noisomeness which breedeth sickness and mortality, all which would be avoided.

The ships would be able to continue longer in the service that they should be appointed unto, and would be able to carry victuals for a longer time.

There is no captain or master exercised in service, but would undertake with more courage any enterprise with 250 able men than with 300 of tag and rag, and assure himself of better success.

The wages being so small causeth the best men to run away, to bribe and make mean to be cleared from the service, and insufficient, unable and unskilful persons supply the place, which discourageth the captains, masters and men, that know what service requireth.

If it shall please her Majesty to yield unto this increase, her High-ness' service would be far safer and much bettered, and yet the charge nothing increased. As for example:

The charge of the *Lion* for one month's wages and victuals of 300 men, after the old rate of 23s 4d per man, doth amount unto £250.

The same ship being now furnished with 250 able men, after the rate of 28s wages and victuals, for every man *per mensem*, will amount unto (even as before) monthly, £250.

The sailors (in consideration of her Majesty's gracious liberality) shall be bound for to bring into the said service, every man his sword and dagger.

Hawkins

From William Cecil, Lord Burghley, to Robert Dudley, Earl of Leicester, 31 March 1586

I am very glad to see a disposition of sending some ships from thence, to impeach the Spanish King, towards his Indies. It is a matter that many years past I did project to the Prince of Orange's Ministers, to have been attempted. We hear that Sir Francis Drake is a fearful man to the King, and that the King could have been content that Sir Francis had taken the last year's fleet, so as he had not gone forward to his Indies. We hear that he hath taken seven rich ships on the coast of the Indies. I wish they were safe in the Thames.

We are here troubled to understand, that from Hambrug (*sic*) and Dantzick, Lubeck, etc. there are a great number of hulks laden for Spain, and do mean to pass about Scotland and Ireland, as some of them did this last year, which they do to avoid all stays in our narrow seas. I would to God your fleet, now intended from those countries, could make a good prize of them; for so should the King of Spain be unable to defend his seas, or to offend any other.

Burghley

In 1584 William, Prince of Orange, the leader of the Dutch in their war of independence against Philip II, had been assassinated by a treacherous palace servant, and, to maintain Dutch resistance after this great loss, Elizabeth had, without declaration of war, sent an army under Leicester to the Netherlands.

Minutes of the Privy Council, 11 May 1586

Whereas of late upon a casual fire happening about the city of Bath the country was like to have risen (the watches of the Beacons near thereabout supposing the same to have been a Beacon fired), they are required to give special charge to such as are and shall be appointed to the ordinary watches of the Beacons in that country generally to make special observance and mark of the Beacons standing upon the coasts of the county, that if any casual fire should happen hereafter in any place thereabout within their view, they may be able to distinguish and discern the same from the Beacon, that they be not deceived and upon needless occasion move the country to rise.

Watchers were stationed on high points, some of them still called beacons, fifteen to thirty miles apart in every county and shire, not just along the coast. They were expected to know, even in the dark, the exact location of the nearest beacons to them, and when they saw one lit, to light their own. In 1588 the system worked most efficiently.

Agent's Report, 15 May 1586

By letters from Biscay which came by Bordeaux
The Bank of Seville is broke.
The Bank of Venice also very likely.
The King of Spain's commandment prohibiting the buying of English commodities.
General speech [gossip] that the King of Spain will make a great army for England of 800 sail of ships but as yet it seem but small preparation, and is only a Spanish brag, and very unlikely in many years for him to provide shipping, mariners, and soldiers for such an army unless the French assist him.

Secret agents were employed by most governments and sometimes sent wildly inaccurate reports.

From Elizabeth I, to the Duke of Parma, 8 July 1586

You may be persuaded that if any reasonable conditions of peace should be offered to us which tend to the establishing of our safety and the honour and liberty of our neighbours, we shall no less will-ingly accept them than unwillingly we have been forced to the contrary, seeing that in no way can we do anything more pleasing to God Almighty than by embracing the peace and safety of Christen-dom of which in these times, we who are princes and monarchs have chiefly to think. And it is known to the Omnipotent (the God of peace and searcher of all human hearts) that to this our heart has always been inclined, to whose judgement we appeal against the malice of those tongues which strive to persuade the world to the contrary.

The Queen

Parma, Philip's viceroy in the Netherlands and son of his illegitimate half-sister Margaret of Parma, had recently been most successful in re-establishing Spanish authority over the Southern Netherlands, where the Protestant revolt had begun. Elizabeth, though she disapproved of rebellion in principle, was willing to support the Dutch and entice Parma into holding up operations in the hope of peace. On the eve of the Armada's sailing she was still sending Parma peace offers.

Minutes of the Privy Council, 23 September 1586

Her Majesty and her Council do greatly stagger at the excessive charge of those wars under his Excellency's [Earl of Leicester's] government for the six months passed.

Minutes of the Privy Council, January 1587

To Sir Owen Hopton, Mr Daniell, Mr Younge
That whereas of late there were discovered certain bad persons who were to be charged with disobedience, misbehaviour and practises against the State and present Government, they are required to examine such persons, especially John Staunghton and Humfrey Fullwood, who were deeplier charged than the rest, and if they should show themselves obstinate and perverse as they have done heretofore, that they should carry them to the Tower, there to be kept close prisoners and to be put to the Rack and torture, to compel them to utter their uttermost knowledge.

Minutes of the Privy Council, January 1587

To Sir Owen Hopton, Sir Edward Waterhouse, knights, William Waad, Thomas Owen and Richard Younge, esquires.
That for as much as Roger Asheton, a companion and a man very inward and greatly trusted by Sir William Stanley [serving with the Spaniards] examined by them upon certain interrogatories where-

unto he wilfully refused to make any answer, they are by their Lordships authorised and willed to put him to the Rack and torture.

*In the sixteenth century the use of torture to obtain information became the
regular practice of many governments. Shakespeare's Portia remarks that
upon the rack men 'do say anything'.*

From a speech by Sir Christopher Hatton, Lord Chancellor, to the
House of Commons, 22 February 1587

It was her Majesty's pleasure to have dangers disclosed. The principal
heads of dangers: The Catholics abroad, the Pope, the King of
Spain, the Princes of the League [in France], the Papists at home
and their Ministers. The principal root hereof: The Council of
Trent, which agreed to extirp Christian religion (which they term
heresy) whereunto divers Princes assented. Pope Pius V sent his
Excommunication against her Majesty, Pope Gregory XIII sends
Jesuits and Seminaries to England and Ireland, and they proceed to
inveigh her subjects and dissuade them from obedience. Pope Sixtus V
imitateth the other Popes . . . The King of Spain's designments
are to invade England and Ireland. His preparations 350 sail of
Spain, 80 galleys of Venice and Genoa, 1 galleass with 600 armed
from the Duke of Florence. 12,000 men maintained by Italy and the
Pope. 6,000 by the Spanish clergy, 12,000 by the nobility and gentlemen of Spain. It is reported that 10,000 of these be horsemen. I think
it not all true, but something there is. We must look to the Papists
at home and abroad; they bring in doctrine of lawfulness and merit
to kill the Queen and have sent their instruments abroad to that
purpose . . .

Concerning Mr Drake's last voyage it was to meet with the
restraints and seizures in Spain and their purpose of war was thereupon discovered, for there was found by the Master of Mr Bond's
ship, who took the Corregidor and others, a Commission from the
King of Spain whereby he termed us his rebels, as he termed the
Low Countries.

*No verbatim records of speeches were made. The above is a reconstruction
from the deputy clerk's notes. Hatton had received many favours from the
queen but had recently given offence by putting the great seal on Mary's death
warrant.*

From the Privy Council, to Sir Francis Drake, 1 April 1587

Her Majesty, for her part, loth for these considerations to exasperate matters further than they are, or to give cause to the world to conceive by any thing that may proceed from her or any of her ministers or subjects that the present alteration between the said King and her is maintained or nourished by her, otherwise than forced thereunto for her own defence: hath commanded us to signify unto you in her name, that her express will and pleasure is you shall forbear to enter forcibly into any of the said King's ports or havens, or to offer violence to any of his towns or shipping within harbouring, or to do any act of hostility upon the land. And yet, notwithstanding this direction, her pleasure is that both you and such of her subjects as serve there under you should do your best endeavour (avoiding as much as may lie in you the effusion of Christians blood) to get into your possession such shipping of the said King or his subjects as you shall find at sea, either going from thence to the East or West Indies or returning from the said Indies into Spain, and such as shall fall into your hands, to bring them into this realm without breaking bulk until her Highness's pleasure shall be further made known unto you in that behalf.

The Privy Council had agreed that Sir Francis Drake should be sent with sixteen ships to attack the Spanish fleet in its ports of assembly. The queen realised that this would be an act of aggression very difficult to excuse and decided at the last minute to stop it. The bearer of the above message, arriving in Plymouth after Drake's departure, took ship but failed, allegedly because of contrary winds, to catch up with the fleet.

From Dr Lobetius, an agent, to Sir Francis Walsingham, 21 April/ 3 May 1587

The Swiss seem none too well united amongst themselves, as some Catholic cantons have separated themselves in order to join the side of Spain.

People talk of great preparations in Spain and Italy against England. The Pope is amassing treasure *exp resentibus futura prospiciens* not withstanding that St Peter said *aurum et argentum non est mecum.*

Strasburg,

Dr Lobetius

From Sir Francis Drake, to John Wooley, Latin Secretary of State, 27 April 1587

Knowing that you, amongst many of my good friends, are desirous to hear of our proceedings in this action, I have thought good to satisfy your expectation with this short advertisement. You shall understand that the 19th of the month we arrived at Cadiz, where, finding divers huge ships loaded with the King's provision for England, of whom we burnt thirty-two, and sank a great argosy, and carried away four with us. We remained in the Road two days, in which time twelve of the King's galleys sundry times encountered us: in which fights we sank two of them, repulsing the residue with very little loss on our parts. Howbeit the ordnance from the shore vehemently thundered at us during our abode there, and the power of the whole country, being raised, resorted in great numbers to their succour, yet (thanked be God) we went thence, in despite of them all, with great honour, being at our departure courteously written unto by one Don Pedro, general of those galleys. Now being well fur-nished with necessary provision, our intent is (God willing) to im-peach the fleet which is to come out of the Straits and divers other places before it join in with the King's forces, in the accomplishment whereof neither willing minds or industry shall be wanting. For want of time I leave the report at large of this good success unto this bearer, and thus in much haste do bid you heartily farewell. From aboard her Majesty's good ship the *Elizabeth Bonaventure,*

Yours, very willing to be commanded,

Drake

There was never heard of so great preparation [as] the King of Spain hath and doth continually prepare for an invasion, yet no doubt but this which God hath suffered us to perform will breed great alteration. Cease not to pray continually, and provide strongly to defend to prevent the worst.

Haste yours,

Drake

From Sir Francis Drake, to John Foxe, 27 April 1587

To my very loving friend Mr John Foxe, preacher, haste and post haste.

Mr Foxe – Whereas we have had of late such happy success against the Spaniards, I do assure myself that you have faithfully remembered us in your good prayers, and therefore I have not forgotten briefly to make you partaker of the sum thereof.

The 19 of April we arrived with Cadiz Road where we found much shipping, but among the rest thirty-two ships of exceeding great burden laden and to be laden with provision, and prepared to furnish the King's Navy, intended with all speed against England; the which when we had boarded and thereout furnished our ships with such provision as we thought sufficient, we burned; and although for the space of two days and nights that we continued there we were still endangered, both with thundering shot from the town and assaulted with the roaring cannons of twelve galleys, we yet sunk two of them and one great argosy, and still avoided them with very small hurt; so that at our departure we brought away four ships of provision to the great terror of our enemies and honour to ourselves, as it might appear by a most courteous letter, written and sent to me with a flag of truce by Don Pedro, general of the galleys. But whereas it is most certain that the King doth not only make speedy preparation in Spain, but likewise expecteth a very great fleet from the Straits and divers other places to join with his forces to invade England, we purpose to set apart all fear of danger and by God's furtherance to proceed by all good means that we can desire you to continue a faithful remembrance of us in your prayers that our present service may take that good effect as God may be glorified. His Church, our Queen and country preserved, and the enemy of the truth utterly vanquished, that we may have continual peace in Israel.

Written by the hand of your obedient son in the Lord, William Spenser, and subscribed with Sir Francis's own hand in this sort.

Your loving friend and faithful son in Christ Jesus,

Drake

[In Drake's own hand] Our enemies are many, but our Protector commandeth the whole world, let us all pray continually, and our Lord Jesus will help in good time mercifully.

Drake

John Foxe, author of a long and highly popular book on the Protestant martyrs, died before receiving this letter. In his youth he had been tutor to Charles Howard, who, as Lord High Admiral, had ordered the raid.

From Vice-Admiral Fenner, to Sir Francis Walsingham, 27 April 1587

The 19 April one hour afore sunset he [Drake] entered the harbour of Cadiz where he was at his [coming in met from] the town with seven galleys, but the same returned soon [whence they came]. In the road there were about sixty ships besides other small vessels which rode under their fortresses, whereof about twenty French ships fled to Port Royal, and some Spaniards whose flight we could not hinder by reason of the schalles [shoals]. At our entry with our shot we sunk one argosy of about 1,000 tons that carried thirty brass pieces, and was very richly laden. There were before night about thirty-eight ships undertaken, and we victors of the road, for the galleys retired to their fortresses. There came presently from St Mary Port two galleys and other two from Port Royal, but in vain, for their chiefest gain was expense of powder and shot.

Of twenty hulks Hollanders confiscate to the King, whose goods were sold to his use, fourteen were fired, and other six escaped to Port Royal; we fired a carrack belonging to the Marquis of Santa Cruz of 1,400 tons. We fired also five great Biscayans, whereof four were lading and taking in of victuals to the King's use for Lisbon, and the fifth being a ship of 1,000 tons was laden for the Indies with iron, spikes, nails, iron hoops and horseshoes.

Also three flyboats of 300 tons laden with biscuit whereof one was half unladen before in the harbour, and there fired; the other two we took away with us.

Some ten barks more laden with wine, raisins, figs, oil, wheat, and such like we fired.

There were by supposition thirty-eight barks fired, sunk, and brought away, which amounted unto 13,000 tons of shipping. There ridd at Port Royal in sight of us by estimation above forty sail, besides those that fled out of Cadiz Roads.

During our abode they gave us small rest by reason of their shot from the galleys, fortresses, and shore, where continually they placed new ordnance at places convenient to offend; which notwithstanding, we continually fired their ships as the flood came in, to the end to be cleared of them; the sight of which terrible fires were to us very pleasant, and mitigated the burden of our continual travail, wherein we were busied two nights and one day in discharging, firing, and lading of provisions, with reservation for good, laudable, and guard-able defence of the enemy.

It pleased God by the general's great care and pains day and night to finish this happy action in her Majesty's service in one day and two nights, and we came out again the Friday in the morning with-out the loss of any one man at the action, or any hurt, but only the master gunner of the *Golden Lion*, whose leg was broken with a great piece from the town, but the man like to do well, God be thanked.

In a small carvell that was taken the night before were five of our men without the general's knowledge because he hastened the enter-prise with all expedition, which was very needful because the sun was not above one hour high at our approach. This carvell being far astern came in very late, so as the galleys intercepted her with much shot and many muskets, but they would never strike, and so was taken, which was all the loss that we sustained.

Ten galleys came forth after us, but as to make sport with their ordnance. At length the wind scanted, and we cast about for the shore and came to anchor within one league of Cadiz, where the galleys suffered us to ride quietly.

Three of those galleys after some sport departed the same day to St Lucar to fetch other three galleys and one galleass that were there, as we understood by advertisement of some of our prisoners.

There were also three flyboats at Malaga laden with bread, and bound for Cadiz, and so for Lisbon. We understand of great pro-vision and forces provided within the Straits; but we doubt not but God, as He hath given us this happy victory to the daunting of the enemy, will also bless this army, and therewith daily cut their forces shorter, to his great annoy, and to the honour of our prince and country, which God for ever continue.

We have now tried by experience the galleys' fight, and I assure you that these her Majesty's four ships will make no account of twenty of them in case they might be alone and not given to guard others.

There were never galleys that had more fit place for their advan-tage in fight; for upon the shot that they received they had present succour from the town which they used sundry times – we riding in a narrow gut, the place yielding no better in that we were driven to maintain the fight until we had fired their ships, which could not be conveniently done but upon the flood, for they might drive clear.

We rest victualled with bread and drink for six months in our ships, and have besides two flyboats full laden with bread sufficient for a good army for three months.

We all remain in great love with our general and in unity throughout the whole fleet.

It may seem strange or rather miraculous that so great an exploit should be performed with so small loss, the place to endamage us being so convenient and their force so great as appeared, from whom were shot at us at the least 200 culverin and cannon shot; but in this as in all others our actions heretofore, though dangerously attempted yet happily performed, our good God hath and daily doth make His infinite power manifest to all papists apparently, and His name be by us His servants continually honoured.

Fenner

Minutes of the Privy Council, July 1587

A letter to the Lord Marquess of Winchester signifying her Majesty's pleasure that (although his purpose was to come to London this Term about his law causes) he should remain in the country, considering the charge his Lordship hath in the counties of Southampton and Dorset, and to give order and direction that the Beacons there on the sea coast and in the country might carefully be watched and looked upon.

From William Cecil, Lord Burghley, to Andreas de Loo, English agent in the Netherlands, 10 October 1587

We have intelligence by many ways out of Spain that there are mighty preparations of a navy *and army* to the seas and most common reports be that this army is presently to come to invade some part of the Queen's dominions; whereby we are in some sort brought to an alarm, and I think her Majesty will be compelled to prepare forces both by sea and land to withstand the same; a matter very impertinent at this time to the furtherance of a peace by treaty. And if you can possibly, I require you to obtain of the Duke presently in writing under his hand, an assurance either of his knowledge that these preparations are not nor shall be meant against any of her Majesty's dominions; or otherwise, if he be not able to assure the same, then at the least that he will by his writing assure her Majesty that he will upon his honour with all expedition send to the King his advice to stay all hostile actions.

From Richmond,

Burghley

Agent's Report, 30 October/9 November 1587

The Prince of Parma's own costly apparel doth exceed for embroidering and is beset with jewels, and the embroiderers and diamond cutters work night and day. There are five hundred velvet coats of one sort for lances, and brave new coats for horsemen. Thirty thousand men are ready and gather in Brabant and Flanders; and in Hennegow and Artois a great number taken up. It is said they shall be in two armies, ten thousand for some great exploit in these parts and twenty thousand to march with the Prince into France. Which way or how soon they shall march is not yet known, but all are ready at an hour's warning.

Antwerp.

From Elizabeth I, to Charles Lord Howard, Lord High Admiral, 21 December 1587

Know ye that we, reposing special trust and confidence in the diligence of our beloved Councillor, Charles, Lord Howard, Baron of Effingham, knight of our illustrious order of the Garter, High Admiral of England, Ireland, Wales, and of the dominions and islands thereof, of the town of Calais and the marches of the same, of Normandy, Gascony and Aquitaine, and Captain General of the Navy and mariners of our said kingdoms of England and Ireland – do, by these presents, assign, make, constitute, ordain, and depute the said Charles to be our lieutenant-general, commander-in-chief, and governor of our whole fleet and army at sea, now fitted forth against the Spaniards and their allies, adherents or abettors. Giving and granting to the same Charles full power and authority to muster, direct, lead, order and command all and singular our vice-admirals, captains, sub-captains, lieutenants, barons, lords, knights, masters of ships, mariners and gunners, and all other soever in our aforesaid fleet and army.

Elizabeth

Howard, a cousin of the Queen and almost her equal in age, had been a friend since boyhood. War had still not been declared against Spain, but his commission was necessary because there was no royal navy in the sense of a fleet of warships ready at all times. The Queen's ships were fitted out for a particular 'service' and their number augmented by privateers and armed merchantmen not in the Queen's pay. For the Armada campaign a host of small ships was also assembled and given various auxiliary duties. Some estimates put the total muster as high as 197 against the Spaniards' 120. The sums sent to the fleet by the Treasury for pay, victuals and other stores were calculated on a monthly basis. This was an endless source of anxiety to the commanders, inclining them to let their ships chase prizes. Everything taken out of a captured vessel was divided between the admiral, captain and crew according to a scale fixed by custom.

From the Lord High Admiral, to William Cecil, Lord Burghley, 24 December 1587

It may be there hath been some report made to your Lordship of some chance that happened here, before my coming down, by fire in one of the ships. I do assure your Lordship it was after this manner. There were two poor knaves that came from Westchester [Chester] that strived for a place to hang up their netting [hammocks] for to lie in, and the one of them had a piece of a candle in his hand, and in striving, the candle fell down where there lay some oakum. It was in the *Elizabeth Bonaventure*; but I hope to make them a warning to others to beware.

Howard

From the Lord High Admiral, to William Cecil, Lord Burghley, 28 February 1588

I protest before God, and as my soul shall answer for it, that I think there were never in any place in the world worthier ships than these are, for so many. And as few as we are, if the King of Spain's forces be not hundreds we will make good sport with them.

And I pray you tell her Majesty from me that her money was well given for the *Ark Raleigh*, for I think her the odd ship in the world for all conditions; and truly I think there can be no great ship make me change and go out of her.

We can see no sail, great or small, but how far soever they be off, we fetch them and speak with them.

From aboard her Majesty's ship the *Ark*.

                                                                        Howard

This ship had been built for Sir Walter Raleigh at Deptford and sold to the Queen for £5,000. What in the design won Howard's praise is not known. She was later renamed Ark Royal.

From John Hawkins, to William Cecil, Lord Burghley, 6 March 1588

There is already taken into the storehouse and provided to the value of £5,000, which is unpaid for; and order given for great cables to be made this winter in Muscovia, for the value of £3,000 which will be most needful.

                                                                        Hawkins

By cultivating good relations with Ivan the Terrible, Duke of Muscovy and Tsar of all the Russias, Elizabeth had ensured direct imports of cables, ropes and pitch. Spanish dockyards were also dependent on supplies from the Baltic countries, which reached them through German ports.

From the Lord High Admiral, to William Cecil, Lord Burghley, 8 April 1588

The *Ark* is arrived this morning here at Margate, wonderfully well trimmed and mended of her leak, which was a bolt forgotten to be driven in, and the outside covered with pitch, so it could not be seen; and when the sea had washed it off, then brake in the leak; and she was not well caulked in any place, but now most perfect.

                                                                        Howard

From the Lord High Admiral, to William Cecil, Lord Burghley, 9 March 1588

On Friday, when the wind came to serve our turns, I sent my son Lewson [Leveson] and three or four gentlemen to them, to make my excuse, and also to visit the Princess of Orange [widow of William the Silent]. My Lord, all the mariners and seamen of Campvere and

Arnemuiden came to the governors and captains and told them that they would serve under me, and be commanded by none but by me; and said whensoever I would send for them, they would come from Count Maurice or any, to me. They of Middelburg heard of it, and they did the like. My Lord, this I dare assure her Majesty, at this hour she is no more assured of the isle of Sheppey to be at her devotion any ways, than she is of the whole isle of Walcheron and all the towns.

Howard

Scale of Pay – Expedition at Sea Anno 1588

The regiment under the charge and conduct of the Lord High Admiral of England – Men 3,868

To himself, *per diem*, £3 6s 8d;
the Lord Henry, Lord Seymour, vice-admiral, £2 *per diem*; Sir John Hawkins, rear admiral, 15s *per diem*; and for the wages of 19 captains at 2s 6d *per diem* apiece, with 22 masters and 3,824 mariners, gunners, and soldiers, and sometimes fewer, serving under them, as the exigent of time and need of service required.

Regiment of Sir Francis Drake, knight – Men 2,737
For himself, being captain and admiral, at 30s *per diem*; Thomas Fenner, vice-admiral, at 15s *per diem*; 28 captains, at 2s 6d *per diem*; 30 masters, and 2,677 other mariners, gunners and soldiers, and sometimes fewer, as services required, serving under them at several times, between the first of January, 1587, unto 10 September, 1588; in all, with £552 9s 9d for conduct in discharge; £3,758 13s 8d for tonnage, and £343 for sea store of sundry merchants of London £19,228 12s 5d.

From William Cecil, Lord Burghley, to the Privy Council, 13 March 1588

    The proportion of victualling to the seas;
    Nota 28 days to 1 month; whereof –
Fish days 10 ⎱ Whereof 4 Fridays that have but 4 meals; so there
Flesh days 16 ⎰ wants 2 days
Fish days – 20 meals
Flesh days – 32 meals

The fare of fish days for every man *per diem*:

Biscuit	1 lb	Beer	[1] gallon.

In fish   1 qr. of stockfish, or the 8th part of a ling.

In cheese, *per diem*, 1 qr. of a pound.

In butter, half qr. *per diem*.

     The flesh day:

Beer and biscuit, *ut supra*.

Flesh, 2 lbs salt beef *per diem*, so as every man hath 1 lb for a meal, and 4 men have 4 lbs for a meal.

     For one day in the week:

A device for bacon for 1 day in a week.

1 lb of bacon for a man *per diem*.

A pint of peas for 1 man for a meal.

1 pottle of peas for 4 men.

4,000 casks will serve for 10,000 men for beer and beef for 3 months.

So there will be 3 days in the week – viz. Sunday, Tuesday and Thursday – for beef; and 3 fish days – Wednesday, Friday and Saturday: and Monday for bacon and peas.

Burghley

The pre-Reformation Friday fast was kept up as a measure of economy welcome to administrators.

From Sir Francis Drake, to Elizabeth I, 13 April 1588

I have received from Mr Secretary some particular notes, and withal a commandment to answer them unto your Majesty.

    The first is that your Majesty would willingly be satisfied from me how the forces now in Lisbon might best be distressed.

    Truly this point is hardly to be answered as yet, for two special causes; the first for that our intelligence are as yet uncertain; the second is the resolution of our own people, which I shall better understand when I have them at sea. The last insample at Cadiz is not of divers yet forgotten; for one such flying now, as Borough did then, will put the whole in peril, for that the enemy's strength is now so great gathered together and ready to invade.

    But if your Majesty will give present order for our proceeding to the sea, and send to the strengthening of this fleet here four more of your Majesty's good ships, and those 16 sail of ships with their

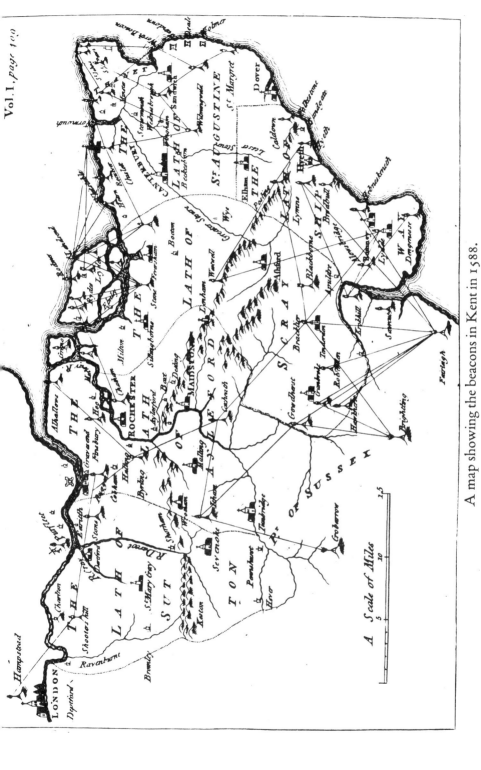

A map showing the beacons in Kent in 1588.

A portrait of William Cecil, Lord Burghley, on a mule.

pinnaces which are preparing in London, then shall your Majesty stand assured, with God's assistance, that if the fleet come out of Lisbon, as long as we have victual to live withal upon that coast, they shall be fought with, and I hope, through the goodness of our merciful God, in such sort as shall hinder his quiet passage into England; for I assure your Majesty, I have not in my lifetime known better men, and possessed with gallanter minds, than together, voluntarily to put their hands and hearts to the finishing of this great piece of work; wherein we are all persuaded that God, the giver of all victories, will in mercy look upon your most excellent Majesty, and us your poor subjects, who for the defence of your Majesty, our religion, and native country, have resolutely vowed the hazard of our lives ...

From Plymouth.
    Your Majesty's most loyal,

Drake

William Borough, second-in-command at Cadiz, and an expert on gunnery and navigation, had withdrawn his ship when she came under fire from a land battery. At the council of war held before the attack he and other captains had, he claimed, been given no inkling of Drake's intentions. This was almost certainly true. Drake, an autocrat who demanded unquestioning obedience, held a court-martial and sentenced Borough to death in his absence, but the Privy Council attached no blame to him and the sentence was not carried out.

From the Lord High Admiral, to William Cecil, Lord Burghley, 28 May 1588

I have received your Lordship's letter, wherein you desire that a certain ship, called the *Mary* of Hamburg, stayed at Plymouth, may be suffered to pass with her lading of rice, almonds, and other goods, to London, whither she is bound.

    Your Lordship shall understand that we have scarcely three weeks' victuals left in our fleet, being bound in by the wind, and watching the first opportunity of the same to go forth unto the seas; and that therefore, for our better provision and prolonging of our victuals, I have caused the said rice to be stayed and taken for her Majesty's use, paying for the same as it is valued at. And for the ship, and the rest of her lading, I will give order that she may pass hence to London, according to your Lordship's request. And so I bid your Lordship most heartily well to fare.

From Plymouth.

Your Lordship's very loving friend to command,

Howard

My good Lord, there is here the gallantest company of captains, sogers [soldiers], and mariners that I think ever was seen in England. It were pity they should lack meat when they are so desirous to spend their lives in her Majesty's sarvis [service].

I pray God all things be in best readiness, if the worst do fall out. And God send us the happiness to meet with them before our men on the land discover them, for I fear me a little sight of the enemy will fear the land men much.

From John Whitgift, Archbishop of Canterbury, to the Bishops of the province of Canterbury, 29 May 1588

You cannot be ignorant of the sundry endeavours in divers parts of this realm, by the lieutenants and others, since the time of these late dangers of foreign invasion by the procurement of the Pope and his adherents, to have had all ecclesiastical men assessed . . . to the finding of horse and other warlike furniture, and to show with others at common musters. We are therefore to remember, and advisedly to weigh with our selves, what dutiful forwardness against these extra-ordinary imminent dangers, of very congruence, is expected at our hands, for the defence of our gracious Sovereign, our selves, our families, and country.

I have lately received letters from my Lords of her Majesty's most honourable Privy Council requiring me in very earnest sort, to move all the Bishops within my province, with what convenient speed may be, effectually to deal with those of their cathedral churches, and other beneficed men in their dioceses; but especially such as be of better standing for the furnishing of themselves with lances, light horses, petronels on horseback, muskets, calivers, pikes, halberds, bills, or bow and arrows, as in regard of their several abilities shall be thought most convenient. I am therefore accordingly hereby to require your Lordship, to whom their abilities are best known, to take a special care, by all good persuasions you can, to move such ecclesiastical persons of your diocese to be ready with all free voluntary provision of man, horse, and furniture, as your Lordship shall think good to allot unto every one to find; and to be showed at some convenient day and place, as you shall thereunto appoint . . . And thus I commit your Lordship to God's holy tuition.

    From Croydon,

        Your Lordship's loving brother in Christ,

                                     Jo.Cant.

As Archbishop, Whitgift presided over the Court of High Commission, which the Queen set up with powers to inflict the death penalty on those who satirised the Church of England. Burghley strongly disapproved of the court's methods of investigation or 'inquisition', as it was then called. The Queen disregarded all such protests, jestingly called Whitgift 'my little black husband', and supported his use of mutilation and capital punishment.

Memorandum to the Privy Council, May 1588

Reasons why the Spaniards should rather land in the Isle of Wight than any other place of England.

If by this preparation of the ships and the galleys, an invasion be intended to any part of England – then, entering into consideration what ports are fittest for his advantage, and most dangerous to work our annoyance, let us look into these ensuing circumstances, and we shall the better judge where he will make his first descent.

Three things he will principally respect.

First, where he may find least resistance, and most quiet landing.

Secondly, where he may have best harbour for his galleys, and speediest supplies out of Spain, France and Flanders.

Thirdly, where he may most offend the realm by incursions, and force her Majesty, by keeping many garrisons, to stand upon a defensive war.

To the first. It carrieth no appearance in reason that he will land in any part of the realm where he shall not be able so soon to put himself on shore, and to intrench himself in strength, but that the whole body and force of that shire, with their neighbouring aids, may and will so disturb him, or prevent him with a battle, that he must either retire to his ships, or hazard his greatest forces and the over⁄throw of his wearied army; we being daily to be reinforced with fresh men and greater supplies; small strength being sufficient to keep them awaking and busied, until a strong head may be made against them.

To the second point. What place can be assigned that may stand indifferent from Spain, Flanders and France, but that they are too remote from the one and too near the other, except the Isle of Wight, Hampton or Portsmouth? To the latter two places, the precedent reason may give cause of security, which holdeth not in the first; but by all winds may be supplied out of one of the three countries before specified.

To the third. There is no doubt to be made, but landing in the Wight – which with an army of 8,000 men, divided into four parts, he may easily do, the force of the Island being unable to resist them with that force – in very short time they may so fortify themselves and possess those parts and places that lie convenient for passing over our supplies, and are by nature more than three parts fortified, that he may keep in safe harbour his galleys to make daily invasions into the firm lands, where they shall perceive the standing of the wind will impeach her Majesty's ships to come to their rescue. So that all the castles and sea towns of Hampshire, Sussex and Dorsetshire will be subject to be burnt, unless her Majesty will keep garrisons in those places, the number and charge whereof will be no less exceeding than how long they shall be forced to continue uncertain.

The Privy Council was attempting to anticipate where the Spaniards would try to land. This adviser took a soldier's view; seamen realised that nothing but a short crossing would suit Parma.

From the Lord High Admiral, to Sir Francis Walsingham, 14 June 1588

We have endured these three days Wednesday, Thursday, and Friday, an extreme continual storm. Myself, and four or five of the greatest ships, have ridden it out in the Sound, because we had no room in Catwater, for the lesser ships that were there; nor betwixt the shore and the Island [Drake's Island], because Sir Francis Drake, with four or five other ships, did ride there. Myself and my company in these ships do continually tarry and lie aboard in all the storm, where we may compare that we have danced as lustily as the gallantest dancers in the Court.

Howard

From Admiral Sir William Wynter, to Sir Francis Walsingham, 20 June 1588

I well remember that in the journey made to Scotland, in the Queen's Majesty's father's time, when we burned Leith and Edinburgh [May 1544], and there was in that expedition 260 sail of ships; and yet we were not able to land above 11,000 men, and we then in fear of none that could impeach us by sea. It may be said the cut between Flanders and the places named is shorter than out of England to the Frith in Scotland, which is true; but, Sir, men that do come for such a purpose, being so huge an army as 30,000 men, must have a mighty deal of all sorts of provisions to serve them, as your honourable wisdom can well consider.

But, Sir, I take the Prince's case to be far otherwise. For I suppose, if the countries of Holland and Zealand did arm forth but only the shipping which the Lord Admiral at his departing delivered unto our admiral in writing that they would send from those parts to join with us here, and that was 36 sail of ships of war, and that it were known to the Prince those did nothing but remain in readiness to go to the seas for the impeaching of his fleet whensoever they did come forth, I should live until I were young again or the Prince would venture to set his ships forth.

We are informed that my Lord Admiral is at Plymouth with his whole army, which is but a bad place for my Lord to be in, if the King of Spain's navy should come. For that wind which would serve to bring them for England, Ireland, or Scotland, will not suffer my Lord to get out.

Wynter

From the Lord High Admiral, to the Privy Council, 22 June 1588

Men have fallen sick, and by thousands fain to be discharged, [and] others pressed in their stead, which hath been an infinite charge [with] great trouble unto us, the army being so great as it is, the ships so many in number, and the weather so extreme foul as it hath been; whereby great charges have risen and daily do. And yet I protest before God we have been more careful of her Majesty's charges than of our own lives, as may well appear by the scantyings [saving by putting six men to a mess instead of four – 'six upon four'] which we have made. And thus leaving to trouble your Lordships any further, I take my leave. From off aboard her Majesty's good ship the *Ark*.

Howard

Agent's Report, 23 June 1588

On Friday last the 20th [Friday was the 21st] of this instant, Sir Francis Godolphin wrote unto my Lord Admiral, that the Thursday before, a bark of Mousehole in Cornwall, being bound for France to lade salt, encountered with nine sail of great ships between Scilly and Ushant, bearing in north-east with the coast of England. Coming near unto them, he, doubting they were Spaniards, kept the wind of them. They perceiving it, began to give him chase. So in the end, three of them followed him so near that the Englishman doubled hardly to escape them.

At his first sight of them there were two flags spread which were suddenly taken in again, and being far off could not well discern the same. They were all great ships, and, as he might judge, the least of them from two hundred tons to five and eight hundred tons. Their sails were all crossed over with a red cross. Each of the greater ships towed astern them either a great boat or pinnace without mast.

From the Lord High Admiral, to Elizabeth I, 23 June 1588

For the love of Jesus Christ, Madam, awake thoroughly, and see the velynous treasons round about you, against your Majesty and your realm, and draw your forces round about you, like a mighty prince, to defend you. Truly, Madam, if you do so, there is no cause to fear. If you do not, there will be danger. I would to God nobody had been more deceived in this than I; it would have been never a whit the worse for your Majesty's service.

I humbly beg your Majesty to pardon me that I do cut off my letter in this sort. I am now in haste, and long to set sail. I beseech the Almighty God to bless and defend your Majesty from all your enemies, and so I do most humbly take my leave. From aboard the *Ark*, ready to weigh, this Sunday night at 12 of the clock.

Your Majesty's most humble and obedient servant,

Howard

This outburst was probably caused by the news that the Queen was still making peace offers to Parma, a piece of subtlety that Howard could not understand.

From Lord Henry Seymour, Admiral of the Channel Fleet, to Sir Francis Walsingham, 26 June 1588

I do what I can to lay in wait for the vessel that should go out of Dunkirk to Spain, but it is a hundred to one she may escape me; yet I think she may sooner fall into the hands of the Lord Admiral; and as yet the wind being so contrary hath retained all the shipping in Dunkirk.

Seymour

Royal Proclamation, 1 July 1588

. . . Her Highness doth by this her Majesty's proclamation straitly charge and command that no person whatsoever shall convey, carry, or bring into any of her Majesty's realms or dominions any of the bulls [by Pope Sixtus V and others], or any transcript or copy thereof, or any of the said libels, books, pamphlets, or writings, nor shall in any wise disperse or utter any of the same. Every such offender shall with all severity be proceeded against and punished according to the martial law by her Majesty's lieutenants in that behalf within the several limits and precincts of their several commissions of lieutenancy, and shall suffer such pains and punishments in that behalf as by the said lieutenants or their deputies by such direction as is aforesaid. And her Majesty is pleased that all such persons as shall apprehend or detect any such offender against this proclamation as is aforesaid, whereby the same offender may be forthcoming to be proceeded upon and to receive punishment according to the quality of the offence, shall have the moiety of all the goods and chattels of the same offender which shall be so apprehended or detected by them. And in case any sheriff, mayor, justice of peace, or other public and inferior officer, or any other to whom it shall or may appertain, shall be found remiss or negligent in the due execution of the proclamation, then the said party or parties so offending shall be brought before the lords and others of her Highness' Privy Council to receive punishment for that remissness and contempt as shall appertain to the nature and quality of the same offence.

Greenwich,

Elizabeth

From William Cecil, Lord Burghley, to Marmaduke Darell, Quartermaster of the Navy, 17 July 1588

There was some fault in you in that you made not your last certificate, which you sent up hither, so perfect as had been requisite, for you neither particularly mentioned the numbers of men, nor the vessels in which they serve so that it may be understood what numbers serve in every of the ships that were with Sir Francis Drake before my Lord Admiral's coming to Plymouth, as also of those numbers supplied by his Lordship after his coming thither.

Burghley

From Marmaduke Darell, Quartermaster of the Navy, to William Cecil, Lord Burghley, 22 July 1588

It hath been, and shall always be most far from me to abuse your Honour with any untrue information. I might well omit the setting down of some ships and men with whom, being not set forth at her Majesty's charge, I had not to do. I do now send you two several notes; the one importing the state of the whole navy, both for the number of ships and men, according to the allowance given, as also for their time of victualling which is now reduced to end all together in all the ships at her Majesty's charge upon 10 August. Only the haste of my Lord Admiral was such in his setting forth upon Saturday morning by reason he had then received some intelligence of the Spanish fleet as that divers of his ships had not leisure to receive the full of their last proportions. And the other note containeth an estimate what money will remain of the last warrant towards the victualling of the 7,079 now at her Majesty's charge from 10 August onwards. In both which notes I have not (I hope) set down anything but what your Lordship will find to be true.

Darell

CHAPTER FOUR

Cold War: Plans and Preparations

Mas héte de improviso que descarga
el contrario furor sobre su pecho.
'Arma, arma; Santiago; arma, arma' grita.
Luego veréis la voz multiplicada,
difusa y repetida en toda boca.
Descripción de un centinela en un campamento
FRANCISCO DE ALDANA. (1547–1578)

(But lo, suddenly the enemy discharges his fury against his breast. 'To arms, to arms! Saint James! To arms, to arms!' he cries. Then you will hear his cry multiplied, spread and repeated in every mouth.)

Philip II, after the vast damage done by Drake to the Spanish colonies in the Caribbean in 1585, began, with characteristic caution, to plan his great enterprise. Nothing short of conquest, it seemed, would end English piracy. His preparations were hurried on after Drake's raid on Cadiz in 1587, which caused a sense of outrage throughout Spain.

The instructions sent to his fleet commander, the Duke of Medina Sidonia, and the commander of the land forces, the Duke of Parma, were elaborate and appear well-considered, but they were drafted without the king having called both men to the palace for joint consultations. Letters from Madrid were at least a fortnight on the road before they reached Parma, and, once the Armada had sailed, ship-to-shore communications became most hazardous. Parma's embarkation could not be undertaken without a prospect of good weather, which was something only seamen could predict, yet Medina Sidonia had no power either to order or cancel it. From the first, Parma seems to have been lukewarm about the invasion plan, partly because his army was a mixed force drawn from almost every nation. He therefore insisted that, as reinforcements, the Armada must bring 6,000 Spanish veterans, a request that added greatly to Medina Sidonia's difficulties over supplies. The soldiers' horses, for example, needed great quantities of water.

In the event, fighting ships, shepherding a great flock of slow, unarmed troop carriers and supply ships, entered the home waters of the most daring seamen in Europe, there to attempt an invasion across the very straits where, as every educated soldier remembered, no less a commander than Julius Caesar had twice failed because summer winds played on exposed beaches crowded with his shipping. Nothing but Quixotic courage and loyalty persuaded seasoned mariners and veteran soldiers to obey Philip's orders.

From Captain Luis Cabreta, to Philip II, October 1580

In this matter of Francis Drake's voyage, I am quite aware that many will be of opinion that it may be remedied with the forces at present at your Majesty's command, with the Portuguese ships and others, and the galleys and galleasses. I might well say the same but I prefer to call it into question.

In conclusion, I wish to say that evils will be sure to happen in the future (since troubles never come singly) and that the sea forces which the enemy can collect are very great, and will increase from day to day, unless some strong effort be made to render your Majesty's present small number of vessels more than equal to the multitude of the enemy. It is all very well to say that your Majesty has 100 galleys. They may be of some little use perhaps in the Mediterranean, but they are of small importance elsewhere and quite unable to redress the evils which may arise, especially on the high seas. It is clear to me that, whilst the expense of them is constant, their utility is only conditional and intermittent.

Captain Luis Cabreta

Drake's voyage, to which Captain Cabreta refers, was his circumnavigation of the world between 1577 and 1580. His secret plan, which he discussed with the Queen, was to enter the Pacific, which no English captain had previously done, and to attack Spanish shipping there. Elizabeth took shares in the venture, and Drake captured vast treasure from a Spanish ship in Peruvian waters. He then went north, laid claim to California, and returned by way of the East Indies and South Africa, bringing home the first load of spices ever to be shipped direct from the Moluccas in an English vessel. Previously the Portuguese had monopolised this trade. While Drake was away, the throne of Portugal fell vacant, and Philip II, who had a strong hereditary claim to it, annexed the country by force of arms. When news of Drake's exploits reached him, he instructed Bernardino de Mendoza, then his ambassador in London, to complain, but Mendoza reported angrily that the Queen spent six hours with Drake hearing the tale of his adventures and paid little attention to Philip's list of grievances. She allowed Drake to keep bullion worth £10,000 without registering the amount.

From the garrison in Castel del Oro, Smerwick, to Philip II, 19 October 1580

The side of his Holiness is sustained by the Earl of Desmond and his brother John of Desmond, and those in their country. In the neighbourhood of Dublin the party is upheld by James Eustace and Feagh MacHugh with other influential persons. Colonel Sebastian St Joseph and the force sent by his Holiness are with the Earl and his brother, who have about 60 horse and 400 foot with 100 arquebusiers. The Colonel has almost 400 foot and munitions.

The affair has proceeded as follows. John of Desmond rose fifteen months ago and the Earl a little over a year, since when they have sustained the war against the Queen. Eustace has been helping us for about three months. Since the Colonel came a fort is building at Smerwick to defend the land and sea and 600 natives have been hired. These pikemen will not serve except at a wage of four gold crowns in coin, and the other soldiers a little more. They wish to be paid in advance. The whole of the population is favourable, and if they saw any strength they would all rise for the cause except the Earl of Ormond, who is the leader of the English and persecutes our party, and Cormac MacTeague, who killed the Earl's third brother.

For the purpose of soliciting the Pope and your Majesty for the aid they require, Friar Matthew de Oviedo is being sent with full powers and information. If all the supplies be sent speedily, it is hoped that the whole of this country may with the help of God be brought to submit to the holy Catholic faith.

From Castel del Oro, Smerwick,

	J. Geraldine
Cornelius Laonenus, Episcopus	James of Baltinglas
Fr. Mateo de Oviedo	Bastian de San Joseph
Nicolaus Sanderus	Alexander Bertoni

From Bernardino de Mendoza, Spanish Ambassador in London, to
Philip II, 11 December 1580

The Viceroy [Lord Grey of Wilton] sent a company of his men to
take possession of the fort on the 10th, and they slaughtered 507 men
who were in it, and some pregnant women, besides which they
hanged seventeen Irish and Englishmen, amongst whom was an
Irishman named Plunkett, a priest, and an English servant of Dr
Sanders. Only a single one of the Lord Deputy's men was injured.
In the fort were found 2,000 corslets, and arquebuses and other
weapons, sufficient to arm 4,000 men, besides great stores of victuals
and munitions, enough to last for months, in addition to money. The
English say that if the fort had held out for four days until Desmond
arrived, the Lord Deputy's retreat would have been cut off, and the
Queen's ships could not have held their own, to the great peril of the
English in Ireland.
  London,

                                                              Mendoza

*The small force that sent out the appeal from Smerwick was obliged to
surrender before help could be sent. They had attempted to start a holy war
against the English. Elizabeth's laws on religion were particularly obnoxious
to the Irish and for most of her reign they conducted a spasmodic guerrilla war
against the English garrisons. In 1577 James Fitzmaurice, brother of the Earl
of Desmond, had gone to Rome to plead with Pope Gregory XIII, who gave
him money. This he used to hire Spanish and Portuguese soldiers of fortune.
After a short-lived success they were trapped in the port of Smerwick in the
far west by the ships of Admiral Sir William Wynter. The massacre which
Mendoza reports was ordered by Captain, later Sir Walter, Raleigh, after
the surrender. The Irish were never given the benefit of the normal customs
of war.*

From Hieronimo Lippomano, Venetian Ambassador in Madrid, to
the Doge & Senate, 29 December 1586/8 January 1587

Every day one hears of fresh preparations for war in various parts of
Spain, and especially in Malaga where forty ovens over and above the
ordinary are at work continually, preparing biscuits to last a year for
a force of 70,000 persons. Francesco Duartes has been charged with
the contract for 30,000 cantaras of cheese [1 cantara = 16 lbs], which

cost 150,000 crowns and were brought by the twenty Hambrug ships which reached Lisbon a few days ago, but as to the real intentions of his Majesty your Serene Highness will discover them more easily from the enclosed report furnished by the Marquis of Santa Cruz, which I have obtained in great secrecy.

Lippomano

Report by the Marquis of Santa Cruz

Learning that many ships have already sailed from England and that others are about to sail, making a total of eighty, his Majesty should put together a fleet and should send it out to seek and fight the English. The galleons of his Majesty in Portugal, and those in the river of Seville, should be got ready, careening and caulking them so that they may be fit for any voyage, however long. Further forty-five great ships which are now lying in Biscaya and Giupuzcoa must be re-fitted, armed, commissioned and victualled for eight months. Considering that the English have done so much damage in so short a time to the merchantmen trading in these waters it is likely that they will do the same to the India fleets; accordingly it would be as well to give orders that at least two more ships beside the Captain and the Admiral should be armed in each fleet; but this is not a reason for dispensing with the escort.

From Giovanni Gritti, Venetian Ambassador in Rome, to the Doge & Senate, 31 December 1586/10 January 1587

His Holiness [Sixtus V] said to me: 'Spain should have attacked England at once; that would have cut off the supplies to Flanders; instead of which much money has been wasted uselessly. We will grant ecclesiastical subsidies of two million to the King of Spain.'

Gritti

From Bernardino de Mendoza, to Philip II, 10/19 April 1587

The English news I send in the general letter are faithfully conveyed to me by the new friend from letters dated the 7th instant. The intelligence sent by my Fleming about the number of ships and men is exactly confirmed.

The friend assures me that Drake has orders to stay as short a time as possible at Plymouth, but that no living soul but the Queen and the Treasurer knew what the design was to be. The Queen would not have even the Lord Admiral informed, as she considers him a frank-spoken man; but, judging from general indications and the haste in sending Drake off, it would seem as if the intention was to try to prevent the junction of your Majesty's fleet, which had to be equipped in various ports, and if they succeed in breaking up a portion of it, then to proceed on the Indian route and encounter the flotillas. To this end they had let out a few words to Drake about Cadiz being a good port to burn the shipping in, if a good fleet were taken thither.

Paris,

Mendoza

From Bernardino de Mendoza, to Philip II, 24 April/3 May 1587

I have no fresh news of Drake since my last, as the weather has prevented passage from England. They write from Rouen under date of 30th ultimo, that a Breton ship reports that Drake had fought with some Biscay ships, and had himself been killed. They were betting 50 to 100 that this was true.

Paris,

Mendoza

From Bernardino de Mendoza, to Philip II, 10/20 June 1587

Owing to the contrary winds that have prevailed lately I cannot give your Majesty any fresher news from England than the 6th. They report that, two days prior to this, Robert Cross arrived in London, having been sent by Drake with two prize ships, which professed to be Italians, one of 800 tons, and the other of 600, loaded with Malvoisie, raisins, and other things which Drake had captured, and which they consider a valuable prize.

This Robert Cross reports that Drake sent him, after entering the Bay of Cadiz, to give an account to the Queen of his voyage, and the fortunes which had attended him on the high seas after he left England. He had encountered a great storm which had scattered his ships, but he had collected them again at the end of five days, after which he had the best weather he could desire and arrived at Cadiz without being discovered. He had there sunk thirty-two ships of 700 and 800 tons each, the smallest of them being 400 tons, and two galleys, he having engaged twelve of the latter which were in port, and done much damage to them. He had also captured six ships, with a great quantity of biscuit, and wine, which was intended for the provisioning of your Majesty's fleet for England. To sum up the tonnage of the ships he had destroyed, he had sunk, burned and captured 25,000 tons burden, and had stocked his fleet with wine and biscuits for six months, and this, he said, would be no small impedi- ment to the junction of your Majesty's fleet. In order to prevent this he would remain on the coast of Spain. I also hear that the General of the galleys in Cadiz sent him a boat load of sweetmeats for his refreshment.

Paris,

Mendoza

From Philip II, to Bernardino de Mendoza, 26 June/6 July 1587

I am very anxious to know if the fourteen ships which you say were being fitted out in England to reinforce Drake have sailed, and whether only the six have arrived, or more; also, what has become of the ten vessels which you report were lying in the Thames ready for sea. The constant repetition of these instructions to you in all the letters, to pay particular attention to these armaments, does not arise from any lack of care in the matter on your part, but because it is of such vast importance that we should have early information of their movements, in order that they may be frustrated; and we are con- strained, therefore, to keep the point before you. By the account we recently sent you of what happened in Cadiz you will see how the matter has been exaggerated in England. I hope in my next to be able to inform you that the Marquis of Santa Cruz has sailed.

Madrid,

The King

An Agreement between the Pope and the King of Spain, 19/29 July 1587

Wherefore if the expedition is made this year 1587, we will contribute one million gold ducats to wit, 500,000 ducats as soon as the royal fleet shall have touched England and the army has been put on land, and the remaining 500,000 ducats in bi-monthly instalments as long as the war lasts in the said island or the kingdom of England has been snatched from its misery.

That if the aforesaid kingdoms of England and Scotland are recovered, as we hope in the Lord they will be, his Catholic Majesty will nominate as king of the said kingdoms someone who will establish and preserve in them the Catholic religion and who will remain grateful to the Apostolic See and accept from it the investiture of the said kingdoms.

From the Duke of Medina Sidonia, to Juan d'Idiaquez, Secretary to Philip II, 6/16 February 1588

I reply to your letters of the 11th. In that which you write to me by his Majesty's orders you inform me that the malady of the Marquis of Santa Cruz has become so serious that but small hope is now entertained of his recovery; and you say how deeply his loss will be felt, as the Armada will be ready to sail by the middle of this month, and to delay its departure will be inadvisable for a host of reasons. His Majesty has therefore, you say, fixed his eyes upon me to take charge of the expedition and to perform the hoped-for great service to God and his Majesty by joining hands with the forces under the Duke of Parma and attacking England; the intention being for the fleet which is being fitted out here to join that at Lisbon under my command. In reply to all this I first humbly thank his Majesty for having thought of me for so great a task, and I wish I possessed the talents and strength necessary for it. But, sir, I have not health for the sea, for I know by the small experience that I have had afloat that I soon become sea-sick, and have many humours. Besides this, your worship knows, as I have often told you verbally and in writing, that I am in great need, so much so that when I have had to go to Madrid I have been obliged to borrow money for the journey. My house owes 900,000 ducats, and I am therefore quite unable to accept the command. I have not a single real I can spend on the expedition.

Apart from this, neither my conscience nor my duty will allow me to take this service upon me. The force is so great, and the undertaking so important, that it would not be right for a person like myself, possessing no experience of seafaring or of war, to take charge of it. So, sir, in the interest of his Majesty's service, and for the love I bear him, I submit to you, for communication to him, that I possess

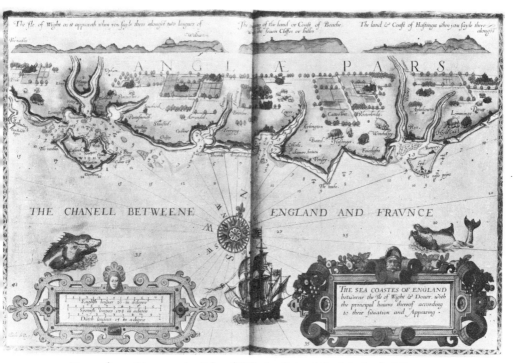

Coast from Kent to the Isle of Wight, from *The Mariner's Mirrour*.

The Escorial with Philip II. Contemporary print.

Philip II, 1527–1598.

neither aptitude, ability, health, nor fortune, for the expedition. The lack of any one of these qualities would be sufficient to excuse me, and much more the lack of them all, as is the case with me at present. But, besides all this, for me to take charge of the Armada afresh, without the slightest knowledge of it, of the persons who are taking part in it, of the objects in view, of the intelligence from England, without any acquaintance with the ports there, or of the arrangements which the Marquis has been making for years past, would be simply groping in the dark, even if I had experience, seeing that I should have suddenly, and without preparation, to enter a new career. So, sir, you will see that my reasons for declining are so strong and convincing in his Majesty's own interests, that I cannot attempt a task of which I have no doubt I should give a bad account. I should be travelling in the dark and should have to be guided by the opinions of others, of whose good or bad qualities I know nothing, and which of them might seek to deceive and ruin me. His Majesty has other subjects who can serve him in this matter, with the necessary experience; and if it depended upon me I should confer the command upon the Adelantado of Castile, with the assistance of the same councillors as are attached to the Marquis. He would be able to take the fleet from here and join that at Lisbon; and I am certain that the Adelantado would have the help of God for he is a very good Christian, and a just man, besides which he has great knowledge of the sea, and has seen naval warfare, in addition to his great experience on land. This is all I can reply to your first letter. I do so with all frankness and truth, as befits me; and I have no doubt that his Majesty, in his magnanimity, will do me the favour which I humbly beg, and will not entrust to me a task of which certainly, I should not give a good account; for I do not understand it, know nothing about it, have no health for the sea, and no money to spend upon it.

The galleons here will sail as soon as the infantry arrive. The Levantine ships will wait for them as the Cape is so infested with corsairs that I have not ventured to let them go. The governor of Algarve writes to me, under date of the 10th, that there were there twenty-two small vessels, and he learns from the captured sailors they had sent ashore that they were expecting Drake this week with thirty ships.

It is of the utmost importance that galleys should go with the

Armada; and it will be well, as you say, to take four of the Spanish galleys for that purpose, or even eight, which, joined with those at Lisbon, would be twelve. They would be of the greatest use and value.

I conclude that in view of the representations I make to you here, his Majesty will permit me not to undertake the voyage. I am incapable of doing so for the various reasons I have stated. I therefore do not reply to your question about the defence of this coast during my absence, as I shall remain here to attend to it myself, and serve his Majesty here as I have always done.

The proposal has been kept secret as you direct, and I send this reply with all speed after commending the matter very earnestly to God.

San Lucar,

Medina Sidonia

Don Alonso Perez de Guzman, 7th Duke of Medina Sidonia, was thirty-seven years old and head of a family owning great estates and tunny fisheries in the region of Cadiz. As Captain General of Andalusia at the time of Drake's raid, he had taken prompt action to protect the town. His excessive modesty concealed great ability and indomitable courage. In his day, as now, wealthy landowners frequently lacked ready money. He was naturally most reluctant to sell ancestral property to help finance an expedition in which he had no confidence.

From Philip II, to the Duke of Medina Sidonia, 22 March/1 April 1588

The undertaking being so important in the service of our Lord which has moved me to collect these forces, and my own affairs depending so greatly upon its success, I have not wished to place so weighty a business in any other hands than yours. Such is my confidence in you personally, and in your experience and desire to serve me, that, with God's help, I look for the success we aim at. In order that you may thoroughly understand my wishes, and be able duly to carry them out, I send you the following instructions:

In the first place, as all victories are the gifts of God Almighty, and the cause we champion is so exclusively His, we may fairly look for His aid and favour, unless by our sins we render ourselves unworthy thereof. You will therefore have to exercise special care that such cause of offence shall be avoided on the Armada, and especially that there shall be no sort of blasphemy. This must be severely enforced, with heavy penalties, in order that the punishment for toleration of such sin may not fall upon all of us. You are going to fight for the cause of our Lord, and for the glory of His Name, and, consequently, He must be worshipped by all, so that His favour may be deserved. This favour is being so fervently besought in all parts that you may go full of encouragement that, by the mercy of God, His forces will be added to your own.

When you receive a separate order from me, you will sail with the whole of the Armada, and go straight to the English Channel, which you will ascend as far as Cape Margate, where you will join hands with the Duke of Parma, my nephew, and hold the passage for his crossing, in accordance with the plan which has already been communicated to both of you.

It is important that you and the Duke should be mutually informed of each other's movements, and it will therefore be advisable that before you arrive thither you should continue to communicate with him as best you can, either by secretly landing a trustworthy person at night on the coast of Normandy or Bologne, or else by sending intelligence by sea to Gravelines, Dunkirk, or Nieuport. You must take care that any messengers you may send by land shall be persons whom you can thoroughly trust; so that verbal messages may be given to them. Letters to the Duke may be sent, those going by sea written in the enclosed cipher, but nothing should be said to the bearers verbally, so that if they be taken they can divulge nothing.

Although it may be hoped that God will send fair weather for your voyage, it will be well, when you sail, to appoint a rendezvous for the whole fleet in case a storm may scatter it. As this rendezvous would have to depend upon the place where the storm overtook you, that is to say, either anywhere near Spain, or at the mouth of the Channel; if it should happen near our own coast, Vigo, Corunna, or the ports in the neighbourhood of Finisterre might be appointed, as the pilots thought best. But if the storm be near the Channel, you will, on consultation with experienced seamen in Lisbon, decide whether the rendezvous should be appointed for the Scilly isles as a port of refuge, or whether it will be better to fix upon a certain latitude at sea. The weather does not promise to be so bad as to prevent the ships from keeping out at sea. In case of your being overtaken by a tempest in the Channel itself, you will likewise discuss with native seamen on the Armada what defenceless port or refuge would serve on the coast of England to shelter the Armada with safety, or whether it would be better to run east or west. But in any case you must keep away from the French and Flemish coasts, in consequence of the shoals and banks.

There is little to say with regard to the mode of fighting and the handling of the Armada on the day of the battle, as they must depend upon circumstances; but I have only to press upon you not to miss the gaining of every possible advantage, and so to order the Armada that all parts of it shall be able to fight and lend mutual assistance without confusion or embarrassement. Above all it must be borne in mind that the enemy's object will be to fight at long distance, in consequence of his advantage in artillery, and the large number of artificial fires with which he will be furnished. The aim of our men on the contrary, must be to bring him to close quarters and grapple with him, and you will have to be very careful to have this carried out. For your information a statement is sent to you describing the way in which the enemy employs his artillery in order to deliver his fire low and sink his opponent's ships; and you will take such precautions as you consider necessary in this respect.

You will be wise enough, in case you gain the victory, not to allow the squadrons of our Armada to get out of hand in their eagerness to chase the enemy. Keep them well together, at least the great mass of them, and give them full instructions beforehand; especially if you have to fight in the Channel, where double care will have to be exercised in this respect, both coasts being unsafe. In such case you will have to fight so as to win.

Disastrous examples have been seen both on land and sea of the effects of over-eagerness in falling to pillage before the victory is absolutely secure. I therefore enjoin you strictly to prevent any disorder arising from this cause, which is apt to produce such terrible results. All hands must continue fighting until the victory is complete, and the benefits will then be secure.

I have ordered the council of war to send you instructions with regard to the distribution of prizes and booty. These instructions must be obeyed; no violation of them can be allowed.

It must be understood that the above instructions about fighting only hold good in case the passage across to England of my nephew the Duke of Parma cannot otherwise be assured. If this can be done without fighting either by diverting the enemy or otherwise, it will be best to carry it out in this way, and keep your forces intact.

If the Armada shall not have had to fight, you will let my nephew have the 6,000 Spaniards you are to give him; but if you have had to engage the enemy, the giving of the men to the Duke will have to depend upon the amount of loss you may have sustained in gaining the hoped-for victory.

In the event of the Duke establishing himself on shore you may station the Armada at the mouth of the Thames and support him, a portion of your ships being told off to hold the passage of reinforce-ments, etc., from Flanders, thus strengthening us on both sides. If circumstances at the time should, in the opinion of the Duke and yourself, render another course desirable you may act in accordance with your joint opinion; but on your own discretion alone you will not land or undertake anything on shore. This you will only do with the concurrence of the Duke, your sole function on your own account being – what indeed is the principal one – to fight at sea.

Whenever in the course of expeditions dissensions have occurred between the commanders they have caused victory to be turned into defeat; and although your zeal for my service leads me to expect from you the loyal co-operation with my nephew the Duke, upon which success depends, I nevertheless enjoin you to keep this point well before you, carrying it out straightforwardly, without varying the design or seeking to interpret it otherwise. I have given to my nephew the Duke similar instructions. You will bear in mind that, if the undertaking be successful, to which result a mutual good under-standing between you will largely contribute, there will be ample honour and glory for both of you; whereas the very reverse will happen in the contrary case, and I hope that for your part you will serve me well in this respect.

You will have to stay there until the undertaking be successfully concluded, with God's help, and you may then return, calling in and settling affairs in Ireland on the way if the Duke approves of your doing so, the matter being left to your joint discretion. In this case you will leave with the Duke the greater number of the Spaniards you take with you and receive in exchange for them such of the Italians and Germans as may be deemed necessary for the task.

Madrid,

The King

From Philip II, to the Duke of Medina Sidonia, 22 March/1 April 1588

When you arrive off Cape Margate, which you must endeavour to do, overcoming the obstacles that may be opposed to you, you will learn where my nephew the Duke wishes you to place the troops with which you are to furnish him, and you will act accordingly. It is my desire that when these troops land they shall be under the command of my Commander-in-Chief of the Light Cavalry of Milan, Don Alonso de Leyva, until the duke takes them over.

Madrid,

The King

From Philip II, to the Duke of Parma, April 1588

If the Armada succeeds, either by means of fighting or in consequence of the unreadiness of the enemy, you will, when the forces from here have arrived to assure your passage across, go over in God's name and carry out the task assigned to you.

But if (which God forbid) the result be not so prosperous that our arms shall be able to settle matters, nor, on the other hand, so contrary that the enemy shall be relieved of anxiety on our account (which God, surely, will not permit) and affairs be so counterbalanced that peace may not be altogether undesirable, you will endeavour to avail yourself as much as possible of the prestige of the Armada and other circumstances, bearing in mind that, in addition to the ordinary conditions which are usually inserted in treaties of peace, there are three principal points upon which you must fix your attention.

The first is, that in England the free use and exercise of our holy Catholic faith shall be permitted to all Catholics, native and foreign, and that those who are in exile shall be permitted to return.

The second is, that all the places in my Netherlands which the English hold shall be restored to me; and the third is that they (the English) shall recompense me for the injury they have done to me, my dominions, and my subjects; which will amount to an exceedingly great sum.

With regard to the free exercise of Catholicism, you may point out to them that since freedom of worship is allowed to the Huguenots in France, there will be no sacrifice of dignity in allowing the same privilege to Catholics in England. If they retort that I do not allow the same toleration in Flanders as exists in France, you may tell them that their country is in a different position, and point out to them how conducive to their tranquillity it would be to satisfy the Catholics in this way, and how largely it would increase the trade of England and their profits, since, as soon as toleration was brought about, people from all Christendom would flock thither in the assurance of safety.

If the principal design should fall through, it would be very influential in bringing them to these, or the best conditions possible, if the Armada were to take possession of the Isle of Wight. If this be once captured, it would be held, and would afford a shelter for the Armada, whilst the possession of it would enable us to hold our own against the enemy. This matter has also been laid before the Duke, so that in case of failure, and if nothing else can be done, you may jointly with him discuss and decide with regard to it.

The King

From the Duke of Parma, to Philip II, 26 March/5 April 1588

Since God has been pleased to defer for so long the sailing of the Armada from Lisbon, we are bound to conclude that it is for His greater glory, and the more perfect success of the business; since the object is so exclusively for the promotion of His holy cause. The enemy have thereby been forewarned and acquainted with our plans, and have made all preparations for their defence; so that it is manifest that the enterprise, which at one time was so easy and safe, can only now be carried out with infinitely greater difficulty, and at a much larger expenditure of blood and trouble.

I am anxiously awaiting news of the departure of the Duke of Medina Sidonia with his fleet, and am confident that your Majesty will have taken care that the expedition shall be as strong and efficient as is necessary in the interest of your service. I am sure also, that your Majesty will have adopted all necessary measures for the carrying out of the task of protecting my passage across, so that not the smallest hitch shall occur in a matter of such vital importance. Failing this, and the due co-operation of the Duke with me, both before and during the actual landing as well as afterwards, I can hardly succeed as I desire in your Majesty's service.

The troops are in their places, and the infantry handy, as I have already assured your Majesty, but the cavalry are much scattered, as there was no more food for them anywhere nearer; and I was obliged to send them to Hainault and Tournoi. I have done, and am doing everything I possibly can to keep them together, and in good heart, knowing as I do how important it is in your Majesty's interest, and how much depends upon it for me personally; but withal the infantry does not exceed 18,000 men, although some Walloons who had gone to their homes are being brought back again.

I humbly beg your Majesty that this matter, so important in the interest of God and your Majesty, shall not be lost sight of. Even if they give me the 6,000 Spaniards from the Armada, as no doubt it is intended to do, my force will still be weak, considering that the enemy will be fully prepared, whilst the sickness and factions that will occur will still further reduce my numbers. It is important, therefore, that no delay or failure should occur on this important point.

Ghent,

Parma

In this letter Parma writes as though he had all the landing craft he needed, since the matter is not mentioned; 18,000 men and their horses would have required weeks of training in embarkation and disembarkation. Other Spanish sources give ample evidence that by July Parma had made no such preparations, and the conclusion must be that he lacked the moral courage to make public his private opinion that the invasion plan was unworkable.

From the Duke of Parma, to Philip II, 27 March/6 April 1588

After I had written the enclosed despatch and was on the point of setting out for Bruges, Dr Rogers, one of the English Peace Commissioners, arrived here. In order to hear him and reply to him, I remained yesterday and today. The object of his visit was to urge with all his strength and eloquence that our Commissioners should first go to Ostend, if only for an hour, and after that the Queen's Commissioners would come unhesitatingly to one of your Majesty's towns. He was politely informed that this was impossible; and that it would be less objectionable for our Commissioners to go to England itself than to one of the towns in these dominions occupied by their troops. The most they could demand was that the negotiations should be conducted in some neutral place, which was the ordinary course under such circumstances; and I said they ought to be contented with the politeness I had shown to the Queen as a lady, in conceding to her the choice of a place, instead of their trying to depart from the arrangement agreed upon. He was very emphatic as to the bad effect that would be produced by the negotiations being abandoned for so trifling a reason as this, and by the war being thus allowed to proceed, to the great injury to Christendom, and the shedding of human blood, particularly as in return for this piece of politeness to the Queen she would not only restore to your Majesty all she holds in these dominions, but would also aid in recovering the portion that still held out.

At last, in order not to break off the negotiations, and to give him some amount of satisfaction, I adopted the expedient of avoiding giving him a decided answer, and said I would send President Richardot to Ostend, who would try to give them all the satisfaction possible. All this makes me suspect that, even if we arrange as to the first meeting where the [letters granting] powers are respectively pro-duced, they will not be satisfied with my authority, and will break off the negotiations, much as I may try to continue them.

Ghent,

Parma

From the Duke of Medina Sidonia, to the Shipmasters of the Armada, 11/21 April 1588

Rations: – Each man is to receive 1½ lbs of biscuit per day, or 2 lbs of fresh bread on the days that biscuit is not served out.

The ration of wine is to consist of a third of an *azumbre* [about 1⅓ pints] of Sherry, or the same of Lamego, Monzon, Pajica, and Condado wine; but only a pint of Candia wine must be served as a ration, that wine being stronger than the others, and it will bear a double quantity of water. The wine to be first used is Condado and Lisbon wine, and then, successively, Lamego and Monzon; Sherry and Candia being consumed last, as those wines bear a sea voyage better. Any pipes of Condado or Lisbon wine that may become spoilt in consequence of being kept will not be credited to you, and you will have to pay for them at the price of Sherry.

On Sundays and Thursdays every man will receive 6 ounces of bacon and 2 ounces of rice. On Mondays and Wednesdays 6 ounces of cheese and 3 ounces of beans or chick peas. On Wednesdays,

Fridays, and Saturdays you will distribute per man 6 ounces of fish, tunny or cod, or, in default of these, 6 ounces of squid, or five sardines, with 3 ounces of beans or chick peas. It must be borne in mind that two different sorts of rations must not be served out on the same day. Oil must be served out on all fish days, one ounce and a half being the ration. Vinegar is to be distributed also on the same days, a quarter of a pint for each ration.

All rations to be served out strictly by the measures and weights which have been supplied to each ship.

Sufficient water must be given to each man for drinking and cooking purposes, but the ordinary water ration must not exceed three pints a day for all purposes, although a larger consumption has been provided for in consequence of the waste that usually takes place by leakage, etc. If any excess in this respect takes place, it may cause serious trouble.

You will carefully inspect the stores constantly, and anything that you see is becoming bad you will serve out at once, nothing else being distributed until that be finished; so that nothing shall be wasted. If any stores be wasted by your negligence you shall pay for them.

You must not serve out more than the ordinary ration to any captain, ensign, sergeant, corporal, or other official; nor to any drummer, fifer, or other without my order. Anything served out in excess will be debited to your account, unless by orders of the Duke or the Provedore Don Bernabe de Pedroso.

Lists to be made of all men on your ship, signed by the Inspector-General and pursers of the fleet; and by these lists you are daily to distribute the rations. In the case of the death or transhipment of any man, his name is to be struck off the list, even though the captain or ensign may claim his ration. Such ration is to be discontinued from the day the man leaves the ship, except by order of the Inspector-General, or purser, of the fleet. Reports must be made every week, if possible, of any reduction of the company on board.

If for any reason, of scarcity or other, rations are omitted or shortened on any day, the ration or quantity short is not to be made up by distribution of a larger quantity on another day. The ship's notary must be present at and take proper account of all distribution of rations, his book to be signed every day by himself and the captain or ensign of infantry on board, or, in their absence, by the sergeant or corporal in charge. The military officer in charge will have to give you vouchers for all stores he may have received from you, specifying the days of receipt and nature of the stores. These vouchers, signed by you and certified by the ship's notary, will then, if in order, and not otherwise, be credited to your stores account.

If the hurry of the embarkation should prevent proper lists of soldiers being made in accordance with the above order, you will give out the rations for the number of men only specified in the certificate signed by me, as the contingent to be shipped on board your vessel. This is, however, only to be done until you can have a proper list drawn up.

In order that the ration oil should not be consumed in the lanterns for the watch, two arrobas [seven gallons] of oil have been served out to you for the lanterns, on the estimate that an arroba a month will be needed for that purpose on ships of 300 tons and up-wards.

Lisbon,

Medina Sidonia

From the Duke of Medina Sidonia, to the President of Finance, 11/21 April 1588

Statement made by Francisco de Valverde of St Lucar, who arrived in this city of Lisbon today, 12 April 1588, as to what he saw in England and London, which place he left on 12 March 1588.

Whilst he was on his way from the Indies, in the flotilla from New Spain under Don Juan Guzman, in the year 1586, on board one of his own ships of 150 tons, four English ships belonging to the Queen, and commanded by John Hawkins, attacked him off Cape St Vincent. He and eighteen of his men were captured with his vessel and cargo of hides and dyewood, and were kept captive for fifteen months. First, they took him to Portsmouth, where he was detained for three months; then to Southampton, where he remained a month, and thence to London where he stayed until 12 March last, when he left for Spain with a passport from the queen. He embarked in the Thames and came by way of Dieppe and Havre de Grace. He states that for the last four months the English have been busy collecting ships from all parts of the kingdom, and that Francis Drake was in London during that time.

He was asked whether there were any Catholics who expected

the coming of the Armada to help them, and replied that a large proportion of the country would join the Spaniards and King Philip; and it was a common saying amongst the people that in this year '88, by God's grace, England would be brought to obedience to the Roman Catholic Church, and they were anxious to see the day.

Medina Sidonia

Agent's Report, 30 April/10 May 1588

Drake has not yet sailed. He is awaiting twenty ships from London and six from Bristol.

He is extremely negligent in guarding his ships; 1,000 of his men have mutinied for want of pay.

In consequence of some news she recently received from Paris, the queen became unwell, and almost had an attack of palpitation of the heart.

From Philip II, to Bernardino de Mendoza, 14/24 April 1588

The Armada I have collected in Lisbon being now ready to sail, and only awaiting a fair wind, I wish to say that it may be that some of the ships, especially the galleys and galleasses, may enter French ports, although they will endeavour to avoid doing so. In such case you will be on the watch, and will arrange that they shall be supplied with what they require in the ports and be allowed to put to sea again at once.

Madrid,

The King

From the Duke of Medina Sidonia, to Philip II, 29 April/9 May 1588

General Summary of the entire Armada

	Ships	Tonnage	Guns	Soldiers	Sailors
Squadron of Galleons of Portugal	12	7,737	347	3,330	1,293
Squadron of Biscay	14	6,567	238	1,937	863
Squadron of Castile	16	8,714	384	2,458	1,719

Squadron of					
Andalucia	11	8,962	240	2,327	780
Squadron of					
Guipuzcoa	14	6,991	247	1,992	616
Squadron of					
Levantine Ships	10	7,705	280	2,780	767
Hulks	23	10,271	384	3,121	608
Pataches and Zabras	22	1,121	91	479	574
Galleasses of Naples	4	—	200	773	468
Galleys	4	—	20	—	362
Oarsmen 2,088	—	—	—	—	—

Duke of Medina Sidonia, Commander-in-Chief.

Don Alonso Martinez de Leyva, Commander-in-Chief of the Cavalry of Milan.

Juan Martinez de Recalde, General of the Biscay fleet, Admiral of the whole Armada.

Diego Flores de Valdes, General of the Galleons of Castile.

Pedro de Valdes, General of the Andalusian fleet.

Miguel de Oquendo, General of the Guipuzcoan fleet.

Martín de Bertendona, in charge of the Levantine ships.

Juan Gomez de Medina, commanding the hulks.

Don Hugo de Moncada, commanding the four galleasses.

Diego Medrano, commanding the four galleys.

Don Antonio Hurtado de Mendoza, General of the despatch boats.
    Lisbon,

                                                            Medina Sidonia

A galleass was a large-oared galley with three masts and a considerable spread of sail. Pataches and zabras were small sailing vessels of the type called pinnace by the English. Galleons were large three-masted men-of-war similar in design and armament to the English, but with higher stern and forecastles, which made them less easy to handle.

From the Duke of Medina Sidonia, to All Ranks, May 1588

First and foremost, you must all know, from the highest to the lowest, that the principal reason which has moved his Majesty to undertake this enterprise is his desire to serve God, and to convert to His church many peoples and souls who are now oppressed by the heretical enemies of our holy Catholic faith, and are subjected to their sects and errors. In order that this aim should be kept constantly before the eyes of all of us I enjoin you to see that before embarking, all ranks be confessed and absolved, with due contrition for their sins. I trust this will be the case with everybody, and that by this means and our zeal to serve God effectually, we may be guided as may seem best to Him in whose cause we strive.

I also enjoin you to take particular care that no soldier, sailor, or other person in the Armada shall blaspheme, or deny Our Lord, Our Lady, or the Saints, under very severe punishment to be inflicted at our discretion. With regard to other less serious oaths, the officers of the ships will do their best to repress their use, and will punish offenders by docking their wine rations; or in some other way at their discretion. As these disorders usually arise from gamb‐ling, you will endeavour to repress this as much as possible, especi‐ally the prohibited games, and allow no play at night on any account.

In order to avoid the troubles that might otherwise arise to this Armada, I hereby proclaim a truce for, and take into my own hands, all quarrels, disputes, insults, and challenges that up to the publica‐tion of these orders may have occurred between any persons, soldiers or sailors of any rank, or other persons whatever, who may be in this fleet, such suspension to last during the whole time of our expedi‐tion, and a month afterwards. The order holds good with all disputes, even those of long standing, and I expressly command that this truce shall on no account be violated, directly or indirectly, under pain of death for treason. As it is an evident inconvenience, as well as an offence to God, that public or other women should be permitted to accompany such an Armada, I order that none should be taken on board. If any attempt be made to embark women, I authorise the captains, and masters of ships to prevent it, and if it be done surreptitiously the offenders must be severally punished.

Every morning at daybreak the ships' boys shall, as usual, say their *Salve*, at the foot of the mainmast, and at sunset the *Ave Maria*. Some days, and at least every Saturday, they shall say the *Salve* with the Litany.

It is of the greatest importance to the success of the Armada that there should exist perfect good feeling and friendship between soldiers and sailors, and that there should be no possibility of quarrels amongst them, or other cause of scandal. I therefore order that no man shall carry a dagger, and that on no account shall offence be given on either side, but that all shall obey their officers. If any scandal should arise, the originator of it shall be severely punished.

When my galleon the *San Martín*, the principal flagship of the fleet, shall fire a signal gun, this will be the order for sailing, and everything will then be at once put in order for immediate departure; so that when the bugle sounds, all the ships may, without delay or confusion, be able to take their places. When I hoist my sails to leave, the rest of the ships will do the same, taking great care to avoid shallows and snags, and carrying the longboats and skiffs ready in case of need. When the ships are out at sea, each one will come to leeward of the flagship to salute and ask for orders; and if it be in the evening to ask for the watchword. They will endeavour to avoid preceding the flagship, either by night or day, and will be very care/ful to keep a good look/out.

The ships will come to the flagship every evening to learn the watchword and receive orders; but as it may be difficult for so many large ships to do this daily without fouling each other, the generals and chiefs of squadrons will be careful to obtain the watchword in good time, so that they may communicate it to the other ships of their respective squadrons. The flagship must be saluted by bugles if there are any on board, or by fifes, and two cheers from the crews. When the response has been given the salute must be repeated. If the hour be late, the watchword must be requested, and when it has been obtained another salute must be given, and the ships will then make way for others.

In case the weather should make it impossible to obtain the watchword on any days, the following words must be employed: –

Sunday, Jesus.	Thursday, The Angels.
Monday, Holy Ghost.	Friday, All Saints.
Tuesday, Most Holy Trinity.	Saturday, Our Lady.
Wednesday, Santiago.	

It is of great importance that the Armada should be kept well together, and the generals and chiefs of squadrons must endeavour to sail in as close order as possible. The ships and pataches under Don Antonio Hurtado de Mendoza will keep next to my flagship, except six of them, two of which will follow Don Pedro de Valdes's flag/ship, two that of Martín de Bertendona, and the remaining two that of Juan Gomez de Medina. These six must be told off at once in order to avoid confusion. Great care and vigilance must be exercised to keep the squadron of hulks always in the midst of the fleet. The order about not preceding the flagship must be strictly obeyed, especially at night.

No ship belonging to or accompanying the Armada shall separate from it without my permission. If any should be forced out of the course by tempest, before arriving off Cape Finisterre, they will make direct for that point, where they will find orders from me; but if no such orders be awaiting them, they will then make for Corunna, where they will receive orders. Any infraction of this order shall be punished by death and forfeiture.

On leaving Cape Finisterre the course will be to the Scilly Isles, and ships must try to sight the islands from the south, taking great care to look to their soundings. If on the voyage any ships should get separated, they are not to return to Spain on any account, the punishment for disobedience being forfeiture and death with disgrace; but are to continue on the course, and endeavour to sight the Scillys from the south. If on their arrival there the Armada be behind them, they will cruise off the place, keeping up to windward, until the Armada appears, or they have satisfied themselves that it had passed them, in which case they will make for Mount's Bay, Saint Michael's between Cape Longnose and the Lizard where instructions will await them if the Armada be not there.

Great care must be exercised in watching the flagship at night, to see whether she alters her course. If she puts about she will first fire a gun, and when she is on her new tack she will show a fresh light on her poop, apart from her lantern. The other ships must acknowledge this by showing an extra light. When the flagship shortens sail she will show two lights, one at the poop, and the other half way up the rigging.

When for any reason she may take in or shorten all her sails, she will show three lights – one astern, one in the rigging, and the other at the maintop. She will also fire a gun for the other ships to do the same. They will answer by numerous lights astern.

If any misfortune should befall any ship at night, which may cause her to take in all her sails, she will fire a great gun, and burn a beacon signal all night, and the other vessels near her will burn many lights, so that she may be seen. They will stand by till daylight, and, if the need be great, will fire another gun.

Don Bernadino de Mendoza, Spanish Ambassador to the French court in 1588.

Antonio de Rego, despen[sero]
del Galeon Sant Martin

Cargo

De los bastim[ent]os que Recive
en [nombre] de la armada de su Mag[esta]d

Cop[i]a de Portugal

Cargo

HaseleCargo a Antonio de Rego desp[ens]ero del
galeon Sant Martin de quatro quintales de viz[co]cho
cocho blanco pesso deCastilla que Recivio
por libranca de 14 de set[iembr]e de 987 Proveedor Ber[nabe]
de Pedrosso en ju[a]n de Mathiauto m[aest]re de la
nave nom[bra]da n[uest]ra s[eñor]a del Pilar de Caragossa.

Vizcocho blanco — 4 q[uintale]s ⅔

Cargan sele mas, seys arrobas y tres quartas de
vinagre dela medida de Cast[ill]a entre s barriles
que por otra libranca deldho Proveedor f[ech]a a
pri[mer]o de dho set[iembr]e deldho año de 987 se le libraro
en el dho maestre.

Vinagre — 6 @ ¾

Cargan sele mas Treynta arrobas de azeyte medida de Castilla enbassado en sessenta botijas
debarro que Recivio enla Ciudad de Punta del-
gada enla Ysla de sant miguel en 13 de
ag[os]to de 1587 las quales se compraron de gaspar
de Brum v[ezin]o dela dha Ciudad para provission
dela g[en]te demar y guerra deldho galeon por
libranca deldho dia.

Azeyte — 30 @

Cargan sele mas dos varadas de Leña que en
18 de ag[os]to deedho año R[ecibi]o en la dha Ciudad [se]
se compraron de Ju[a]n R[odrigu]es v[ezin]o della
por libranca deldho dia.

Leña — 2 Var[ad]as

Men of quick sight will be always stationed at the masthead on the look-out, particularly at sunrise and sunset, and they must count the sails of the Armada. In the event of their discovering any in excess, the main topsail will be twice dipped and a gun fired, when the ships near will give chase and overhaul the intruders, so that they may not escape. Any captain whose negligence allows such a ship to get away will be punished. If, however, the flagship gives the signal by gunfire for the ships to rejoin, they will do so, even though they are on the point of capturing the intruder.

When any number of sails up to four be sighted by a ship, she will take in her maintopsail, hoist a flag over her maintopsail yard, and fire a gun; but if she discovers a greater number of sails than four she will hoist a flag to her mainmast head, take in her maintopsail, and fire two guns in succession, trying to give notice to the flagship. When the latter perceives the signals the ship will resume her position.

When a ship sights land ahead, she will signal by taking in both of her topsails at the same time. If land ahead be sighted by a ship at night, she will fire a gun and put her bows to seaward, burning two lights at her poop. Those who perceive the signals will also put about on the same tack, showing two lights astern.

When the flagship has anything to communicate, she will hoist a flag at the poop, near the lantern, and the other ships will then approach to help her, the rest of the ships doing the same.

Great care must be taken to extinguish the galley fire before sunset.

The soldiers must allow the rations to be distributed by those appointed for the duty, and must not themselves go down and take or choose them by force, as they have sometimes done.

The sergeant or some other company officer must be present at the distribution to prevent disorder. The rations must be served out early, so that supper shall be finished before nightfall.

Let no ship under my command dare to enter port or cast anchor until the flagship has first done so, unless by my written order, on pain of exemplary punishment.

The military officers must see that the soldiers' arms are kept clean, ready for service; and, in any case, must cause them to be cleaned twice a week. They must also exercise their men in the use of their arms, so that they may be expert when needed.

During the voyage orders will be given with regard to the duty of each man in an engagement, but I order that great care be taken that the bombardiers have ready the usual buckets and tubs full of vinegar and water, and all the customary preparations of old sails, and wet blankets, to protect the ships against fire thrown upon them.

The same care must also be exercised that there are plenty of balls made ready, with the necessary powder and fire match; and that the soldiers are supplied by the magazine keeper with the proper weight of ammunition as ordered for each ship.

I also order that the soldiers' quarters be kept clear of boxes and other things, and that truckle beds are not to be allowed in any of the ships. If any such exist they are to be demolished immediately, and I order the sailors not to allow them. If the infantry possess them let the sailors inform me thereof, and I will have them removed.

As the mariners have to attend to the working of the ship their quarters should be the fore and poop castles, out of the way of the soldiers who might embarrass them. They are to retain these quarters during all the voyage.

The cannon must be kept in good order, loaded with ball, and near each piece must be placed its magazine with ammunition. Let great care be taken with the cartridges of each piece, to avoid their taking fire, and let the loaders and spongers be near at hand.

Each ship, according to its tonnage and artillery, will carry the half pipes necessary, to be filled with water on the day of battle, when they will be distributed between the pieces and the upper works, as may be advisable. Near them should be kept some old rags or blankets, to wet and stifle any fire that may break out. The artificial fire should be entrusted to the most experienced men, to be used when necessary. If this is not confided beforehand to men who understand the management of it, great damage may result.

By the same rule that no ship is to precede the flagship, particularly at night, no vessel is to lag behind it. Let each ship sail according to her speed and burden, as it is very important that the Armada should keep together. This is urged very particularly upon captains, masters and pilots.

A copy of these instructions signed by me and countersigned by my secretary, will be sent to each ship of the fleet, and will be publicly read by the notary on board; in order that sailors and soldiers alike may be informed of them, and not plead ignorance. The said notaries are ordered to read these instructions three times a week publicly, and to obtain due testimony that they have done so. Any neglect of this shall be severely punished.

All this must be publicly made known, and inviolably obeyed. In the interests of his Majesty's service no infraction whatever is to be allowed of any portion of these orders, or otherwise the offenders shall be well punished at our discretion.

On board the galleon *San Martín*, off Belem,

Medina Sidonia

An Exhortation by Medina Sidonia [not issued]

The saints of Heaven will go in our company, and particularly the holy patrons of Spain; and those of England itself, who are perse-cuted by the heretics, and cry aloud to God for vengeance, will come out to meet us and aid us, as well as those who sacrificed their lives in establishing our holy faith in the land, and watered it with their blood. There we shall find awaiting us the aid of the blessed John Fisher, Cardinal-Bishop of Rochester, of Thomas More, of John Forrest, and of innumerable holy Carthusians, Franciscans, and other religious men, whose blood was cruelly shed by King Henry, and who call to God to avenge them from the land in which they died. There, too, shall we have the help of Edmund Campion, of Ralph Sherwin, of Alexander Briant, of Thomas Cotton, and many other venerable priests and servants of the Lord, whom Elizabeth has torn to pieces with atrocious cruelty and exquisite torments. With us too, will be the blessed and innocent Mary, Queen of Scotland, who, still fresh from her sacrifice, bears copious and abounding wit-ness to the cruelty and impiety of this Elizabeth, and directs her shafts against her. There also will await us the groans of countless imprisoned Catholics, the tears of widows who lost their husbands for the faith, the sobs of maidens who were forced to sacrifice their lives rather than destroy their souls, the tender children who, suckled upon the poison of heresy, are doomed to perdition unless deliverance reaches them betimes; and finally myriads of workers, citizens, knights, nobles, and clergymen, and all ranks of Catholics, who are oppressed and downtrodden by the heretics, and who are anxiously looking to us for their liberation.

With us go faith, justice, and truth, the benediction of the Pope, who holds the place of God on earth, the sympathies of all good people, the prayers of all the Catholic Church; we have them all on our side. God is stronger than the devil, truth stronger than error, the Catholic faith stronger than heresy, the saints and angels of Heaven stronger than all the power of hell, the indomitable spirit and sturdy arm of the Spaniard stronger than the drooping hearts and lax and frozen bodies of the English. One thing alone remains, gentlemen: Let there go with us too a pure and clear conscience, a heart inspired alone with love and zeal for the glory of the Most High; the single thought to fight first for our holy faith, for our law, our King, and our country. Let us live Christian lives, without offence towards our God, in brotherhood with our fellow soldiers, and in obedience to our captains. Courage! steadfastness! and Spanish bravery! for with these the victory is ours, and we have nought to fear.

From the Duke of Parma, to Philip II, 3/13 May 1588

I am informed by your Majesty's letters that your Armada, under the Duke of Medina Sidonia was quite ready to sail, and am rejoiced to hear that it is coming so well provided with men, and everything else necessary. I assure myself that this must be the case, as nothing less could be expected from your Majesty's great experience and prudence, knowing, as your Majesty does, how very much depends upon this point. I am anxiously looking from hour to hour for news of the Duke, as I do not think he can fail to send soon, to assure me that I shall be duly supported.

I note that there will be no failing with regard to the 6,000 effective Spaniards which the Duke is to give me, and I am sorry that, for the reasons your Majesty lays down, he will not be able to let me have any more. The Spaniards must be our right arm in this business, and we have very few of them here, although the veterans of them are the best in the world; so that in the interest of the success of the enter-prise I wish the number could be increased. We are short of good pilots and even of seamen. If the passage were a long one we could not venture upon it.

The Count of Olivares has sent me from Rome a discourse and declaration drawn up in English by Allen, with the object referred to, in order that it may be printed and spread over England at the time of the invasion. It shall first be translated, so that we may see whether there is anything to suppress or add to it, and it shall then be printed in the form of a short proclamation, containing the principal heads of the discourse, as Allen himself agrees. I have no doubt that Allen's aid, both in the important religious questions, and in other political affairs, will be extremely advantageous, seeing his great influence amongst the Catholics, and his goodness, efficiency, and learning.

Bruges,

Parma

From the Duke of Medina Sidonia, to Philip II, 4/14 May 1588

The Armada took advantage of a light easterly wind, which blew for a few hours on the 11th instant, to drop down the river to Belem and Santa Catalina, where the ships now only await a fair wind to sail. God send it soon! On the 11th Captain Francisco Morosini came to me with a letter of credence from the Duke of Parma, dated in Ghent the 22 March. His message is to the effect that the Duke sends him to ascertain the present state of the Armada, and to inform me of the Duke's preparations in Flanders. He had less troops than I expected, as this man tells me they will not exceed 17,000 all told, with 1,000 light horse, and 300 small vessels, but none with oars or top masts.

On the galleon *San Martin*,

Medina Sidonia

From the Duke of Medina Sidonia, to Philip II, 18/28 May 1588

With regard to your Majesty's orders as to reinforcing the Duke of Parma with men, I will act in accordance with what I can learn of the strength of the enemy, and the opportunity that may offer for meeting and defeating him at sea, before any operations are attempted on land. The opinions of those whom I have consulted here is that the best course would be to break up the enemy's sea force first. When this be done, as I hope, by the help of God, it will be if the enemy will meet me, the rest will be safe and easy.

If I find no obstacle in the way, I will not divide the Armada or seek the enemy, but will push forward to join hands with the Duke of Parma. In case, as your Majesty says, that Drake with his fleet should fortify himself at Plymouth, or any other port, in order to let me pass on, and then come out and attack me at sea, between his fleet and their other one which they have sent against the Duke, I have taken every precaution, as will be seen by the formation I have ordered to be adopted. Either of the two horns of our formation, with their supports, and two of the galleasses which accompany the first four ships, would be able to cope with one of the enemy's fleets.

The weather is not good, and a NNW wind is blowing, but I have sent some ships down the river, and some more went down today with a great deal of trouble. They are at anchor on the bar. If a land wind blows tomorrow morning I will go down with the rest of the fleet. Not an hour has been, or shall be lost.

On the royal galleon,

                                                    Medina Sidonia

From the Duke of Parma, to Philip II, 29 May/8 June 1588

I am almost in despair for want of money, as your Majesty has ordered that the 670,000 ducats I expected should be employed for the account of the Armada. I have already expended the 300,000 from the Duke of Mantua; 100,000 has been given to the Duke of Lorraine and his friends, and 200,000 from Juan Ortiz has been spent on victuals, etc. I have now only the 100,000 received from Sicily, and the loss on exchange reduces that sum to 87,500. Without money we shall be ruined.

Bruges,

                                                              Parma

From the Duke of Medina Sidonia, to the Duke of Parma, 31 May/ 10 June 1588

I am equally anxious to have the joy of saluting your Excellency soon, both for the pleasure it will give me personally, and because our junction must precede the execution of his Majesty's plans. He has ordered me not to turn aside, and even if I am impeded simply to clear the way, and proceed to join hands with you, advising you when I reach the English coast, so that with a knowledge of my whereabouts your Excellency may bring out your fleet. I greatly wish the coast were capable of sheltering so great a fleet as this, so that we might take some safe port to have at our backs; but as this is impossible, it will be necessary to make the best use we can of what accomodation there may be, and that your Excellency, as soon as Captain Morosini arrives (which will depend upon the weather), should come out and meet me, sending back to me the zabra that takes the captain, with advice as to your position, and where we may meet.

I have called together the pilots and practical seamen on the Armada who know the whole of the English coast, and consulted them as to which ports on that coast could accomodate the Armada in safety from storms. The unanimous decision was that in certain states of the weather set forth in the document taken by Captain Morosini, the ships might be safe in Gouchepe and Harlage [un-identified], and even Dover, but that with a SW or SSW wind, we should not be below Cape [Margate]. I have told them that everything will depend upon the weather, and the most important point will be to effect a junction between this Armada and your Excellency's fleet. When this be done I trust that, with God's help, all will proceed in accordance with our desires in His service.

What I fear most in the Armada is lack of water. It is true that we carry a six months' supply, but I do not see where we can obtain any more, and it will be advisable for your Excellency at once to consider how we may be aided in this respect, even if it be necessary to trans-port water in boats from Dunkirk, unless your Excellency knows of any port where both shelter and water may be obtained for the Armada, which would be a very great point gained. In any case it will be necessary for your Excellency to have all the butts that can be obtained got ready and filled with water to send to the Armada as soon as it arrives. I have given full details of this and other points to Captain Morosini, who will inform you thereof.

On the royal galleon,

Medina Sidonia

From the Duke of Medina Sidonia, to Philip II, 11/21 June 1588

I expected that on the morning after I entered port with a part of the Armada, the rest would have come in, as it was too late for them to enter that evening. During that night, however, and the next day the weather became so heavy that it is believed that the ships have put to sea. The people of the country say that so violent a sea and wind, accompanied by fog and tempest, have never been seen; and it is very fortunate that all the Armada was not caught outside, and particularly the galleys, which would certainly have been wrecked, and the whole Armada endangered. We should have been scattered, and many lost, and it would have been days before we could have united again. Fortunately, however, part of the fleet is here, and the rest will know that they have to join me here. The weather is now moderating, and I expect the ships will now make for this port; so that I hope, in two or three days, to send your Majesty a statement of what has happened. I am very sorry that the bad weather of yesterday has separated the fleet, which will be disabled, and all will have to be watered afresh.

Many men are falling sick, aided by the short commons and bad food, and I am afraid that this trouble may spread and become past remedy.

On the galleon *San Martín*, port of Corunna,

Medina Sidonia

From the Duke of Parma, to Philip II, 12/22 June 1588

... The Duke will learn clearly from my letters that I cannot depart in the slightest degree from the plan laid down, or from your Majesty's express orders; to the effect that the enemy being fully prepared and awaiting us as they are, not only must there be no mistake about my having the 6,000 Spaniards, but it would greatly add to the probable success of the enterprise if I could have a much larger number. With regard to my going out to join him he will plainly see that with these little, low, flat boats, built for these rivers and not for the sea, I cannot diverge from the short direct passage across which has been agreed upon. It will be a great mercy of God, indeed, if, even when our passage is protected and the Channel free from the enemy's vessels, we are able to reach land in these boats. As for running the risk of losing them by departing from the course agreed upon, and thus jeopardising the whole undertaking, if I were to attempt such a thing by going out to meet the Duke, and we came across any of the armed English or rebel ships, they could destroy us with the greatest of ease. This must be obvious, and neither the valour of our men nor any other human effort could save us.

Bruges,

Parma

This letter, containing Parma's first hint that he was unprepared, arrived after the Armada's departure.

From the Duke of Medina Sidonia, to Philip II, 14/24 June 1588

Your Majesty ordered me to go to Lisbon to fit out this Armada and take charge of it. When I accepted the task I submitted to your Majesty many reasons, in the interest of your service, why it was better that I should not do so. This was not because I wished to refuse the work, but because I recognised that we were attacking a kingdom so powerful, and so warmly aided by its neighbours, and that we should need a much larger force than your Majesty had collected at Lisbon. This was my reason for at first declining the command, seeing that the enterprise was being represented to your Majesty as easier than it was known to be by those whose only aim was your Majesty's service.

Nevertheless, matters reached a point when your Majesty ordered me to sail, which I did, and we have now arrived at this port scattered and maltreated in such a way that we are much inferior in strength to the enemy, according to the opinion of all those who are competent to judge. Many of our largest ships are still missing, as well as two of the galleasses; whilst on the ships that are here there are many sick, whose number will increase in consequence of the bad provisions. These are not only very bad, as I have constantly reported, but they are so scanty that there cannot be more than sufficient to last two months. By this your Majesty may judge whether we can proceed on the voyage, upon the success of which so much depends. Your Majesty has embarked in this expedition all your resources both in ships and warlike stores, and I can see no means whatever of redressing any disaster that may befall us.

I recall the great force your Majesty collected for the conquest of Portugal, although that country was within our own boundaries, and many of the people were in your favour. Well Sire, how do you think we can attack so great a country as England with such a force as ours is now? I have earnestly commended this matter to God, and feel bound to lay it before your Majesty, in order that you may choose the course best for your service whilst the Armada is refitting here. The opportunity might be taken, and the difficulties avoided, by making some honourable terms with the enemy. Your Majesty's necessities also make it meet that you should deeply ponder before-hand what you are undertaking, with so many envious rivals of your greatness.

Corunna,

Medina Sidonia

From Philip II, to the Duke of Medina Sidonia, 25 June/5 July 1588

I now come to your letter enclosing the report and opinion of the council you summoned. With regard to the suggestion that the Armada should leave Corunna for the purpose of seeking along the coast for the missing ships, that should not be adopted on any account. The missing ships should join you there, and when all, or a sufficient number, are united, you may proceed on your expedition, and I approve of the orders you had sent out to this effect.

The stores you have – enough, as you report for two months – are very considerable, besides what you may take on board at Corunna, and the supplies which will be sent after you, and provided for you in Flanders. [Added in the king's own hand] But you must take great care that the stores are really preserved, and not allow yourself to be deceived, as you were before.

San Lorenzo,

The King

Report by Ensign Esquivel, 25 June/5 July 1588

On Friday, 1 July, at daybreak we sighted St Michael's Bay and Cape Longnose, five or six leagues distant. The general opinion was that, being so near the land, we should hardly fail to catch a fisher-boat during the night. The wind then rose in the SW, with heavy squalls of rain, and such a violent gale that during the night we had winds from every quarter of the compass. We did our best by con-stant tacking to keep off the land, and at daybreak the wind settled in the N, and we tried to keep towards Ireland in order to fulfil our intention; but the wind was too strong, and the sea so heavy that the pinnace shipped a quantity of water at every wave. We ran thus in a southerly direction, with the wind astern blowing a gale, so that we could only carry our foresail very low. At four o'clock in the after-noon, after we had already received several heavy seas, a wave passed clean over us, and nearly swamped the pinnace. We were flush with the water, and almost lost, but by great effort of all hands the water was baled out, and everything thrown overboard. We had previously thrown over a pipe of wine and two butts of water. We lowered the mainmast on to the deck, and so we lived through the night under a closely reefed foresail.

On Sunday we were running under the foresail only, and at nine o'clock in the morning we sighted six sails, three to the N, and three to the SE, although they appeared to be all of one company. We ran between them with our foresail set, and two of those on the SE gave us chase. We then hoisted our mainmast and clapped on sail, and after they had followed us until two o'clock, they took in sail and resumed their course. At nine o'clock we sighted another ship lying to and repairing, with only her lower sails set.

On Monday, 4 July, we sighted land off Rivadeo.

From Hieronimo Lippomano, to the Doge & Senate, 27 June/7 July 1588

The commander-in-chief announces that the provisions of the Armada, designed for eight months, are already almost all consumed and gone bad; and that he had been obliged to throw overboard a great quantity of biscuits, cheese, and salt meat which was quite putrid. New provisions accordingly are required, and already two officers have left for Galicia and the Asturias with ample authority to requisition all the provisions in those kingdoms; to take them on board, to try the guilty; the contractor, Francesco Duarte, being especially blamed for the bad biscuits.

His Majesty has suspended all payments of any sort soever for two months, even salaries, with the exception of those which affect the Armada. There is some grumbling, especially as they fear that the two months may be spread over the whole period of this campaign. The campaign is costing just now upwards of one million in gold a month.

Madrid,

Lippomano

From Hieronimo Lippomano, to the Doge & Senate, 2/12 July 1588

The Duke of Medina Sidonia has issued orders forbidding, upon pain of death, any information about the Armada to be sent to anyone. This causes great difficulty in procuring news; all the same I am informed that the departure of the Armada cannot take place for many days, and that many ships are lying in the ports of Galicia too badly damaged to be able to join the rest of the fleet. They whisper that more than one ship is actually lost; though the Duke writes to the King that they are all safe in the ports of Galicia.

    Madrid,

Lippomano

From Admiral Juan Martinez de Recalde, to Philip II, 1/11 July 1588

I have not been able to help him [Medina Sidonia] much lately in consequence of an attack of sciatica, but thank God the remedies applied have been efficacious, and I arose today without pain. The Duke came to see me yesterday and we discussed at length the sailing of the expedition. He seems to be much vexed at having to hurry the departure. I showed him how important speed was for the attainment of the object. He is in great fear that the stores and provisions which are being collected here will not be got together in time to supply the needs of the Armada. Profiting by the permission which your Majesty and Don Juan give me in your letter of the 5th instant I will state my own opinion on the matter.

    So far as I understand, the object of the Armada is to meet and vanquish the enemy by main force, which I hope to God we shall do if he will fight us, and doubtless he will.

    In the contrary case we have to proceed to the Downs, and there join hands with the Duke of Parma's force in Dunkirk, whose passage across we are to protect to the most convenient point which may be agreed upon. This point should be the nearest possible one on either side of the Thames.

    This will take some little time, as in the case of there being a cavalry force, as I understand there will be, it cannot be carried over in one passage, and we shall be fortunate if it can be done in two.

    After this be done the first thing will be to obtain a port for the Armada. If it be found possible to obtain anchorage and shelter in the river itself, supported by the army, no other reinforcements will be needed; or at least those from Flanders will suffice. I imagine from what I can see, however, that Flanders will be much exhausted, and the help from there inconsiderable. From the mouth of the Thames to Southampton – about forty leagues – I know of no port capable of taking large vessels, all the coast being very uninviting. The harbours of Southampton and the Isle of Wight are well defended by forts, and it appears to me that the most convenient and easiest ports for landing would be Falmouth, Plymouth, or Dartmouth, especially as the highly necessary reinforcements of men and stores will have to be sent from Spain, and isolated vessels will be exposed to much danger from the enemy higher up the Channel.

I see, nevertheless, the objection to separating the Armada from the land force. Of the two difficulties I do not presume to judge which is the lesser.

In the case of our encountering and defeating the enemy, I feel sure that he will not suffer so much damage as to be unable to repair, at all events sufficiently to impede the passage of our reinforcements high up the Channel. But it will be difficult for him to do this if our Armada be stationed in the above-mentioned ports lying nearest to Spain. If it be possible for the reinforcement to be sent in strength sufficient to attack those ports, whilst the conquest is being effected higher up, that will be the best course. In that case, after the army of Flanders had been taken across and strengthened, the Armada might return towards Ushant and meet the reinforcements with which it might enter one of the said ports, and then either push a force inland towards the Bristol Channel, or form a junction with the other army.

Corunna,

Recalde

From the Duke of Parma, to Philip II, 8/18 July 1588

I am greatly grieved at receiving no news of the Duke of Medina Sidonia and the Armada, although vague rumours of all kinds continue to reach us. I pray God fervently to bless the enterprise, which is undertaken in His cause, and which I cannot persuade myself He will allow to fail.

The troops of all nationalities, both horse and foot, are in their places, mustered near the places of embarcation, as I have already informed your Majesty. Thank God the health is generally good, and the men full of spirits worthily to serve God and your Majesty.

Bruges,

Parma

From the Duke of Medina Sidonia, to Philip II 9/19 July 1588

The 400 Galician soldiers sent by the Count of Lemos, and some that came from Monterey, are so useless that they are no good, even for pioneers. Besides this they are nearly all married and have large families; and are, indeed, absolutely unserviceable old men. Their wives have been coming in with their troubles and lamentations to such an extent that it goes against my conscience to ship the men. The captains themselves have refused to have anything to do with them, as it is evident that all the use they would be is to die on board the ships, and take up space. Not a soul of them knows what an arquebus is, or any other weapon, and already they are more dead than alive; some of them have not eaten anything for two days. Under the circumstances, therefore, I have thought it best to send them all away and they have gone to their homes.

Corunna,

Medina Sidonia

From the Duke of Parma, to Philip II, 10/20 July 1588

The troops are in the field, and we are on the eve of the execution of the task we have in hand, and yet at the last moment we may have to break up from sheer necessity. What account can I give of the fleet, of stores, artillery, and all the rest, unless some resources reach me from somewhere or in some form?

Bruges,

Parma

CHAPTER FIVE

War: Victory

This England never did, nor never shall,
Lie at the proud foot of a conqueror . . .
Come the three corners of the world in arms,
And we shall shock them.

King John V vii 112

The English nearly lost the war on the first day. When on Saturday, 20/30 July, the Armada was sighted off the Lizard, one squadron was operating in the Straits of Dover under Lord Henry Seymour, who reported 'Such summer season saw I never the like, what for storms and variable winds', while Howard, Drake and the bulk of the fleet lay cooped up in Plymouth Sound. The wind was in the south-west and, had the enemy attacked, Howard would have been most vulnerable. Drake, knowing in an instant that he could not put to sea before nightfall, perhaps made a show of finishing a game of bowls to conceal his anxiety. It was without doubt a great feat of seamanship to warp the ships out and get to windward before daylight. Their superior speed and fire-power were quickly apparent, and after the battle Howard was criticised for not pressing home his attacks. The best reply to this was given by Sir Walter Raleigh in his History of the World:

'The Lord Admiral was better advised than a great many malignant fools that found fault with his demeanour. The Spaniards had an army aboard them, and he had none; they had more ships than he had, and of higher building and charging, so that, had he entangled himself with those great and powerful vessels, he had greatly endangered this kingdom of England. But our admiral knew his advantage and held it.'

Howard, in his dispatch of 29 July, made the same point with his customary bluntness:
'Their force is wonderful great and strong, yet we pluck their feathers by little and little.'

His fleet was divided into four squadrons, his own and those of Drake,

Hawkins and Frobisher. The winds were mainly light, and the Armada's eastward passage was slow. A series of running fights developed. After one of these the San Rosario, crippled by a collision, was left behind. It was Drake's Revenge that seized her and held her company to ransom. Sir Francis had behaved like a pirate, determined that his crew should return home, as on previous occasions, fittingly rewarded. Frobisher was furious, and swore that during the night Sir Francis had extinguished his poop light, which the fleet was following, and put about to make the capture before rejoining the admiral.

Dispatches from the fleet made more and more urgent pleas for fresh supplies of powder and shot. These were ferried out from many south coast ports, but were still insufficient. For every cannon ball fired an almost equal weight of powder had to be expended. To shorten range made gunfire more effective, but risked envelopment in the enemy mass, and being shot at by musketeers or boarded by swarms of hardy fighters armed with pikes and swords.

The crisis of the battle came after a week. The Armada was lying at anchor in Calais Road, a position swept by wind and strong currents. Howard's council of war decided to send to Dover for fireships. Then to save time, eight vessels already in the fleet were sacrificed. As the burning hulks drifted towards them, the Spaniards feared a mighty explosion and slipped their cables. In the confusion one big ship's rudder was broken and she drifted ashore.

The most severe fighting of the campaign occurred next day off Gravelines and many Spanish ships were damaged by gunfire. Two were wrecked on the Nieuport and Blankenberghe sands, where they were looted by the Dutch. When the strong wind had nearly driven the rest of the Armada on to the Ruytingen shoals, it suddenly shifted to the south and made possible escape in the direction of Scotland. The English fleet, though its ammunition and victuals were exhausted, followed until it was thirty leagues east of Newcastle, and then turned for home. At first the English commanders did not realise how great a victory they had won, and there was much speculation about the Armada's probable course.

From the Lord High Admiral, to Sir Francis Walsingham, 6 July 1588

Being here in the midst of the Channel of the Sleeve, on Friday being the 5th of the month, I received your letter of 28 June, and another

Charles, Lord Howard of Effingham, 1536–1624, Lord High
Admiral, Privy Councillor, and from 1597, Earl of Nottingham.
Inset left, the Armada fight; inset right, the fight at Cadiz in 1596.

Sir Francis Drake, 1540–1596.

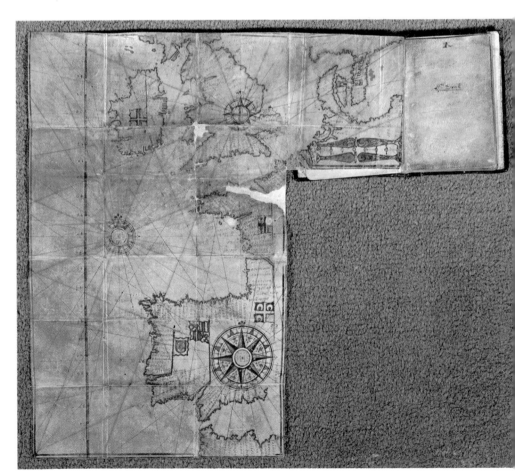

Drake's pocket map of the English and Spanish coasts.

of the same date, which was written after you had made up your packet.

The cause of the long time that these letters were in coming unto me was, because the pursuivant embarking himself upon the Monday at Plymouth, was fain to beat up and down the sea with a contrary wind until Tuesday, before he could find me.

By your first letter, I find how greatly you stand assured, that neither the French King, nor the havens and port towns, that stand for the King, will give any help or assistance unto the Spanish army. As for New Haven [Le Havre], it is not a place that can serve their turns ...

I am sure you have seen the letter which I sent unto her Majesty, of the discovery of certain of the Spanish fleet not far off Scilly, which made me to make as much haste out to sea as I could; for upon Sunday our victuals came to us, and having the wind at north-east, I would not stay the taking in of them all; but taking in some part of them, I appointed the rest to follow with me, and so bore to Scilly, thinking to have cut off those Spanish ships seen there, from the rest of their fleet; but the wind continued not sixteen hours there, but turned south south-west, that we were fain to lie off and on in the Sleeve, and could go no farther.

Then did I send Sir Francis Drake, with half a score ships and three or four pinnaces, to discover. In his way, hard about Ushant, he met with a man of mine, whom I had sent in a bark, ten days before to lie off and on there for discovery, who had met with an Irish bark, and staid her, which had been on the 22nd taken by eighteen great ships of the Spanish fleet, sixteen leagues south south-west of Scilly. They had taken out of the said bark five of her most principal men, and left in her but three men and a boy. One of the greatest Spanish ships towed her at her stern by a cable, which in the night time, the wind blowing somewhat stiff, broke, and so she escaped in the storm. This did assure us greatly, that the Spanish fleet was broken in the storm afore; and, by all likelihood, we conjectured, if the wind had continued northerly, that they would have returned back again for the Groyne; but [considering the] wind hath served these six or seven days [we] must look for them every hour if they mean to come hither.

Sir, I send a fine Spanish carvell on, eight days agone, to the Groyne to learn intelligence, such a one as would not have been mistrusted; but when she was fifty leagues on her way, this southerly wind forced her back again unto us. Therefore I pray you, if you hear or understand of any news or advertisement by land, that I may hear of them from you with expedition.

I have divided myself here in three parts, and yet we lie within sight of one another; so as if any of us do discover the Spanish fleet, we give notice thereof presently the one to the other, and thereupon repair and assemble together. I myself lie towards Ushant; and Mr Hawkins, with as many more, lieth towards Scilly. Thus are we fain to do; or else, with this wind, they might pass by, and we never the wiser. Whatsoever had been made of the Sleeve, it is another manner of thing than it was taken for. We find it by experience, and daily observation, to be an hundred miles over: a large room for me to look unto ... From aboard her Majesty's good ship the *Ark*.

Your assured loving friend,

Howard

Minutes of the Privy Council, 8 July 1588

To the Deputy Lieutenants of Kent.
Whereas their Lordships find by the report made unto them by Sir John Norris, knight, how necessary it were for the withstanding of such attempts as may be made by the enemy to have certain places fortified there within that county, as namely Little Joy near to Sandwich, the towns of Sandwich and Canterbury and a sconce to be made within the Isle of Sheppey at a place over against the King's Ferry, their Lordships nothing doubt but that you will deal very effectually with the inhabitants for the speedy execution thereof.

From Lord Henry Seymour, to Sir Francis Walsingham, 12 July 1588

Such summer season saw I never the like; for what for storms and variable unsettled winds, the same unsettleth and altereth our determinations for lying on the other coast, having of late sundry times put over, with southerly winds, so far as Calais; and suddenly enforced, still with westerly great gales, to return to our English coasts, where, so long as this unstable weather holdeth, and that the same serveth well many times for the Spaniards to come yet shall they be as greatly dangered by the raging seas as with their enemies.

Seymour

From the Lord High Admiral, to Sir Francis Walsingham, 17 July 1588

I have heard that there is in London some hard speeches against Mr Hawkins because the *Hope* came in [to] mend a leak which she had. Sir, I think there were never so many of the prince's ships so long abroad, and in such seas, with such weather as these have had, with so few leaks; and the greatest fault of the *Hope* came with ill grounding before our coming hither; and yet it is nothing to be spoken of. It was such a leak that I durst have gone with it to Venice.

Howard

From Sir Francis Drake, to Lord Henry Seymour, 21 July 1588

I am commanded by my good Lord, the Lord Admiral, to send you the carvel in haste with these letters, giving your Lordship to understand, that the army of Spain arrived upon our coast the 20th of the present, and the 21st we had them in chase; and so coming up to them, there had passed some common shot between some of our fleet and some of them; and as far as we can perceive, they are determined to sell their lives with blows. Whereupon his Lordship hath commanded me to write unto your Lordship and Sir William Wynter, that those ships serving under your charge should be put into the best and strongest manner you can, and ready to assist his Lordship, for the better encounting of them in those parts where you now are ... Written aboard her Majesty's good ship the *Revenge*, off of Start, this 21st, late in the evening 1588.

Your Lordship's poor friend ready to be commanded,

Drake

PS This letter my honourable good Lord is sent in haste. The fleet of Spaniards are somewhat above a hundred sails, many great ships. But truly, I think not half of them men of war. Haste.

Your Lordship's assured,

Drake

From the Lord High Admiral, to Sir Francis Walsingham, 21 July 1588

I will not trouble you with any long letter; we are at this present otherwise occupied than with writing. Upon Friday, at Plymouth, I received intelligence that there were a great number of ships descried off of the Lizard; whereupon, although the wind was very scant, we first warped out of harbour that night, and upon Saturday turned out very hardly, the wind being at south-west; and about three of the clock in the afternoon, descried the Spanish fleet, and did what we could to work for the wind, which [by this] morning we had recovered, descrying their f[leet to] consist of 120 sail, whereof there are four g[alleasses] and many ships of great burden.

At nine of the [clock] we gave them fight, which continued until one. [In this] fight we made some of them to bear room to stop their leaks; notwithstanding we durst not adventure to put in among them, their fleet being so strong. But there shall be nothing either neglected or unhazarded, that may work their overthrow.

Sir, the captains in her Majesty's ships have behaved themselves most bravely and like men hitherto, and I doubt not will continue, to their great commendation. And so, recommending our good success to your godly prayers, I bid you heartily farewell. From aboard the *Ark*, thwart of Plymouth.

Your very loving friend,

Howard

Sir, the southerly wind that brought us back from the coast of Spain brought them out. God blessed us with turning us back. Sir, for the love of God and our country, let us have with some speed some great shot sent us of all bigness; for this service will continue long; and some powder with it.

To celebrate the Armada victory a medal was cast showing warships on a raging sea with the legend FLAVIT JEHOVAH ET DISSIPATI SUNT *(God blew and they were scattered). This was done for Prince Maurice of Nassau, the Dutch commander-in-chief.*

On the obverse was the Protestant Church built on a rock in the midst of stormy waters with the legend ALLIDOR NON LAEDOR *(I am assaulted but not wounded). See illustration facing page 145.*

From the Lord High Admiral, to the Earl of Sussex, 22 July 1588, a postscript.

Since the making up of my letter there is a galleass of the enemy's taken with 450 men in her; and yesterday I spoiled one of their greatest ships, that they were fain to forsake it.

I pray your Lordship send her Majesty word hereof with speed, as from me. The captain's name is, as I hear say, Don Pedro de Alva, general of the field.

The messenger saith that there is an hundred gentlemen in the galleass which was taken, who for the most part were noblemen's sons.

Howard

From Lord Henry Seymour, to the Privy Council, 23 July 1588

May it please your Lordships: I mean not to trouble you with many lines, because I do send your Lordships the original, Sir Francis Drake's letter [to Seymour 21 July] by which you shall understand the state of the Spanish army, how forward they be; and to our opinions here, we conjecture still their purpose may be to land in the Isle of Wight, to recover the same – which God forbid. Thus humbly praying your Lordships to send us powder and shot forthwith, whereof we have want in our fleet, and which I have divers times given knowledge thereof, I humbly take my leave. From aboard the *Rainbow*, at anchor a quarter seas over against Dover, 23 July 1588, at 11 of the clock at night.

Our victuals do end the last of this month; yet upon extremity, now we know the enemy at hand, we will prolong that little we have as long as we can.

Your Lordships' humbly to command,

Seymour

I do send forthwith to the fleets of Zealand and Holland, to wish them to repair unto us. Also I have made the Lieutenant of Dover acquainted therewith, to the end he may have a better care thereof.

Dutch co-operation was limited to using shallow-draft ships to prevent any attempt by barges to bring Parma's army out to join the Armada.

From Richard Pitt, Mayor of Weymouth and Melcombe Regis, to the Privy Council, 24 July 1588

I have received letters from the Right Honourable the Lord High

Admiral of England, advertising unto me that his Lordship hath taken two great carracks or ships from the enemy, sent to the shore, wherein is great store of powder and shot in either of them; and requireth that all the said powder and shot be sent unto his Lordship with all possible expedition, for that the state of the realm dependeth upon the present supply of such wants.

Richard Pitt, Mayor

From Robert Dudley, Earl of Leicester, to Sir Francis Walsingham, 25 July 1588

We have here news commonly spread abroad that my Lord Admiral hath taken either admiral or vice-admiral and the great galleass besides one great ship sunk. The Almighty God be praised therefore, and to give further victory, to his glory and the comfort of his poor church, as no doubt it must be, with the greatest renown and perpetual fame to her Majesty that ever came to any prince. And this being true, I would gladly know what her Majesty will do with me. I have here now assembled in camp 4,000 footmen, as gallant and as willing men as ever was seen; with the horse yet only of this shire. The lying in camp will do them much good, though it be but for a short time; and in my poor opinion, not good to dismiss them over suddenly, though the fleet be defeated, till ye see a little also what Parma will do.

Leicester

From Sir Francis Walsingham, to William Cecil, Lord Burghley, 26 July 1588

I find by a letter written from my Lord Admiral unto her Majesty that, for lack of powder and shot, he shall be forced to forbear to assail and to stand upon his guard until he shall be furnished from hence. There is twenty-three last of powder sent unto him with a proportion of bullet accordingly.

I hope there will be an hundred sail of Hollanders and Zealanders at the least to assist the Lord Admiral within these three days.

Walsingham

From Robert Dudley, Earl of Leicester, to Elizabeth I, 27 July 1588

My most dear and gracious Lady! It is most true that these enemies that approach your kingdom and person, are your undeserved foes, and being so, hating you for a righteous cause, there is the less fear to be had of their malice or their forces; for there is a most just God that beholdeth the innocency of your heart; and the cause you are assailed for is His and His church's; and He never failed any that faithfully do put their chief trust in His goodness. He hath, to comfort you withal, given you great and mighty means to defend yourself; which means, I doubt not but your Majesty will timely and princely use; and your good God that ruleth all, will assist you and bless you with victory.

It doth much rejoice me, to find, by your letter, your noble disposition, as well in present gathering your forces, as in employing your own person in this dangerous action. And because it pleaseth your Majesty to ask mine advice touching your army, and to acquaint me with your secret determination for your person; I will plainly and according to my poor knowledge, deliver my opinion to you. For your army, it is more than time it were gathered, and about you, or so near you, as you may have the use of it upon a few hours warning; the reason is, that your mighty enemies are at hand, and if God suffer them to pass by your fleet, you are sure they will attempt their purpose in landing with all expedition.

Now for the placing of your army; no doubt but I think, about London, the meetest for my part; and suppose others will be of the same mind; and that your Majesty do forthwith give the charge thereof, to some special nobleman about you; and likewise do place all your chief officers; that every man may know what he shall do; and gather as many good horses, above all things, as you can, and the oldest, best, and assuredest captains, to lead; for therein will consist the greatest hope of good success, under God. And as soon as your army is assembled, that they be, by and by, exercised, every man to know his weapon; and that there be all other things prepared in readiness for your army, as if they should march upon a day's warning; especially carriages, and a commissary of victuals, and your master of ordnance. Of these things, but for your Majesty's commandment, others can say more than I, and partly there is orders already set down.

Now for your person, being the most dainty and sacred thing we have in this world to care for, much more for advice to be given for the direction of it, a man must tremble when he thinks of it; specially finding your Majesty to have that princely courage, to transport yourself to the utmost confines of your realm, to meet your enemies and to defend your subjects. I cannot, most dear Queen, consent to that; for upon your well doing consists all the safety of your whole kingdom; and therefore preserve that above all. Yet will I not that, in some sort, so princely and so rare a magnanimity should not appear to your people and the world as it is. And thus far, if it please your Majesty, you may do, to draw yourself to your house at Havering; and your army being about London, at Stratford, East Ham, and the villages thereabout, shall be always not only a defence, but a ready supply to these counties, Essex and Kent, if need be. And in the mean time, your Majesty, to comfort this army, the people of both counties, may, if it please you, spend two or three days to see both the camp and the forts. It is not above fourteen miles at most from Havering, and a very convenient place for your Majesty to lie by the way, and so rest you at the camp. I trust you will be pleased with your lieutenant's cabbin; and within a mile there is a gentleman's house, where your Majesty may also be. You shall comfort not only these thousands, but many more that shall hear of it. And thus far, but no farther, can I consent to adventure your person. And by the grace of God, there can be no danger in this, though the enemy should pass by your fleet. But your Majesty may without dishonour return to your own forts being but at hand; and you may have two thousand horse, well to be lodged at Rumford and other villages near Havering; and your footmen to lodge near London.

From Gravesend, ready to go to your poor, but most willing soldiers.

Leicester

From the Lord High Admiral, to Sir Francis Walsingham, 29 July 1588

I have received your letter wherein you desire a proportion of shot and powder to be set down by me and sent unto you; which, by reason of the uncertainty of the service, no man can do; therefore I pray you to send with all speed as much as you can. And because some of our ships are victualled but for a very short time, and my Lord Henry Seymour with his company not for one day, in like to pray you to dispatch away our victuals with all possible speed, because we know not whether we shall be driven to pursue the Spanish fleet.

This morning we drove a galleass ashore before Calais, whither I sent my long boat to board her, where divers of my men were slain, and my lieutenant [Amyas Preston] sore hurt in the taking of her. Ever since we have chased them in fight until this evening late, and distressed them much; but their fleet consisteth of mighty ships and great strength; yet we doubt not, by God's good assistance, to oppress them; and so I bid you heartily farewell. From aboard her Majesty's good ship the *Ark*.

Your very loving friend,

Howard

I will not write unto her Majesty before more be done. Their force is wonderful great and strong; and yet we pluck their feathers by little and little. I pray to God that the forces on the land be strong enough to answer so present a force. There is not one Flushinger nor Hollander at the seas. I have taken the chief galleass this day before Calais, with the loss of divers of my men; but Monsieur Gourdan doth detain her, as I hear say. I could not send unto him, because I was in fight; therefore I pray you to write unto him, either to deliver her, or at leastwise to promise upon his honour that he will not yield her up again unto the enemy.

From Sir Francis Drake, to Sir Francis Walsingham, 29 July 1588

This bearer came aboard the ship I was in in a wonderful good time, and brought with him as good knowledge as we could wish. His carefulness therein is worthy recompense, for that God hath given us so good a day in forcing the enemy so far to leeward as I hope in God the Prince of Parma, and the Duke of Sidonia shall not shake hands this few days; and whensoever they shall meet, I believe neither of them will greatly rejoice of this day's service. The town of Calais hath seen some part thereof, whose Mayor her Majesty is beholden unto. Business commands me to end. God bless her Majesty, our gracious Sovereign, and give us all grace to live in his fear. I assure your Honour this day's service hath much appalled the enemy, and no doubt but encouraged our army. From aboard her Majesty's good ship the *Revenge*.

Your Honour's most ready to be commanded.

Drake

There must be great care taken to send us munitions and victual whithersoever the enemy goeth.

Drake

From Robert Cecil, to William Cecil, Lord Burghley, 30 July 1588

My duty remembered to your Lordship: Although this bearer's letter to Mr Secretary will thoroughly advertise your Lordship, yet with remembrance of my duty, I thought good to acquaint you with that which I have heard of a Spanish gentleman taken yesterday in one of the galleasses, which was run ashore at Calais, and there is seized by Monsr. Gourdan. The captain of this ship, named Moncada, one of the greatest personages in the fleet, was killed with a small shot of a musket that pierced both his eyes. The second of account in that ship is taken and kept in one of the ships in her Majesty's fleet. This man that is here is a proper gentleman of Salamanca, who affirmeth that there is great lack imputed to the Duke of Parma, in that he hath not joined with this fleet which hath lingered about Calais and Gravelines of purpose for him, and would not have stirred from those roads, if the device of the fireworks on Sunday had not forced them to slip their anchors and so make head away, in which instant my Lord Admiral gave them that fight which we saw upon the land yesterday; where, as terrible as it was in appearance, there was few men hurt with any shot, nor any one vessel sunk. For, as this man reporteth, they shoot very far off; and for boarding, our men have not any reason.

Your most obedient son,

Cecil

From Richard Tomson, Lieutenant of the *Margaret and John* of London, to Sir Francis Walsingham, 30 July 1588

It pleased my Lord Admiral to appoint certain small ships to be fired on Sunday about 12 of the clock at night, and let drive with the flood amongst the Spaniards; which practice, God be thanked, hath since turned to our great good; for it caused the Spaniards to let slip their anchors and cables, and confusedly to drive one upon another; whereby they were not only put from their roadstead and place where they meant to attend the coming of the Duke of Parma, but did much hurt one to another of themselves; and now by the earnest pursuit of our Englishmen, very much weakened and dispersed, the Lord be praised; so that of the 124 sail that they were in Calais Road, we cannot now find by any account above 86 ships and pinnaces; so that I cannot conjecture but by the furious assault that my Lord and his associates gave them early on Monday morning, and did continue in vehement manner eight hours, hath laid many of them in the bottom of the sea, or else run with the coast of Flanders to save their lives, though unpossible to save their great ships, by reason of their evil harbours.

My Lord Admiral, seeing he could not approach the galleass with his ship, sent off his long boat unto her with fifty or sixty men, amongst whom were many gentlemen as valiant in courage as gentle in birth, as they well showed. The like did our ship send off her pinnace, with certain musketeers, amongst whom myself went. These two boats came hard under the galleass sides, being aground; where we continued a pretty skirmish with our small shot against theirs, they being ensconced within their ship and very high over us, we in our open pinnaces and far under them, having nothing to shroud and cover us; they being 300 soldiers, besides 450 slaves, and we not, at the instant, 100 persons. Within one half hour it pleased God, by killing the captain with a musket shot, to give us victory above all hope or expectation; for the soldiers leaped overboard by heaps on the other side, and fled with the shore, swimming and wading. Some escaped with being wet; some, and that very many, were drowned. The captain of her was called Don Hugo de Moncada, son to the viceroy of Valencia. He being slain, and the seeing our English boats under her sides and more of ours coming rowing towards her some with ten and some with eight men in them, for all the smallest shipping were the nearest the shore, put up two handkerchers [handkerchiefs] upon two rapiers, signifying that they desired truce . . .

Richard Tomson

From Sir Francis Drake, to Sir Francis Walsingham, 31 July 1588

I am commanded to send these prisoners ashore by my Lord Admiral; which had, ere this, by me been done, but that I thought their being here might have done something, which is not thought meet now. Let me beseech your honour, that they may be presented unto her Majesty, either by your honour, or my honourable good Lord my Lord Chancellor, or both of you. The one, Don Pedro, is a man of great estimation with the King of Spain, and thought next in this army to the Duke of Sidonia. If they should be given from me unto any other, it would be some grief to my friends. If her Majesty will have them, God defend, but I should think it happy.

We have the army of Spain before us, and mind, with the grace of God, to wrestle a pull with him. There was never any thing pleased better, than the seeing the enemy flying with a southerly wind to the northwards.

God grant we have a good eye to the Duke of Parma; for, with the grace of God, if we live, I doubt it not, but ere it be long, so to handle the matter with the Duke of Sidonia, as he shall wish himself at St Mary port, among his vine trees.

God give us grace to depend upon Him; so shall we no doubt victory; for our cause is good. Humbly taking my leave, this last of July, 1588.

Your honour's faithfully to be commanded ever,

Drake

I crave pardon of your honour for my haste, for that I had the watch this last night upon the enemy.

Drake

From Sir John Hawkins, to Sir Francis Walsingham, 31 July 1588

The Spaniards take their course for Scotland; my lord doth follow them. I doubt not, with God's favour, but we shall impeach their landing. There must be order for victual and money, powder and shot, to be sent after us.

Hawkins

Sir John, whose improvements in the design of warships and in naval administration had contributed greatly to victory, was knighted for his services during the campaign. The Lord High Admiral knighted Martin Frobisher at the same time.

From Admiral Sir William Wynter, to Sir Francis Walsingham, 1 August 1588

Upon Sunday, being the 28th day, my Lord put out his flag of council early in the morning, the armies both riding still; and after the assembly of the council it was concluded that the practice for the firing of ships should be put in execution the night following, and Sir Henry Palmer was assigned to bear over presently in a pinnace for Dover, to bring away such vessels as were fit to be fired, and materials apt to take fire. But because it was seen, after his going, he could not return that night, and occasion would not be over slipped, it was thought meet that we should help ourselves with such shipping as we had there to serve that turn. So that about 12 of the clock that night six ships were brought and prepared [signalled to] with a saker shot, and going in a front, having the wind and tide with them, and their ordnance being charged, were fired; and the men that were the executers, so soon as the fire was made they did abandon the ships, and entered into five boats that were appointed for the saving of them. This matter did put such terror among the Spanish army that they were fain to let slip their cables and anchors; and did work, as it did appear, great mischief among them by reason of the suddenness of it. We might perceive that there were two great fires more than ours, and far greater and huger than any of our vessels that we fired could make, and about 9 of the clock in the morning we feat [fetched] near unto them, being then thwart of Gravelines. They went into a proportion of a half moon. Their admiral and vice-admiral, went on each side, in the wings, their galleasses, armados of Portugal, and other good ships, in the whole to the number of sixteen in a wing, which did seem to be of their principal shipping. My fortune was to make choice to charge their starboard wing without shooting of any ordnance until we came within six score of them, and some of our ships did follow me. The said wing found themselves, as it did appear, to be so charged, as by making of haste to run into the body of their fleet, four of them did entangle themselves one aboard the other. One of them recovered himself, and so shrouded himself among the fleet; the rest, how they were beaten. I will leave it to the report of some of the

Spaniards that leapt into the seas and taken up, and are now in the custody of some of our fleet.

The fight continued from 9 of the clock until 6 of the clock at night, in the which time the Spanish army bare away NNE and N by E, as much as they could keeping company one with another, I assure your Honour in very good order. Great was the spoil and harm that was done unto them, no doubt. I deliver it unto your Honour upon the credit of a poor gentleman, that out of my ship there was shot 500 shot of demi-cannon, culverin, and demi-culverin; and when I was furthest off in discharging any of the pieces, I was not out of the shot of their arquebus, and most times within speech one of another. And surely every man did well; and, as I have said, no doubt the slaughter and hurt they received was great, as time will discover it; and when every man was weary with labour, and our cartridges spent and munitions wasted – I think in some altogether – we ceased and followed the enemy, he bearing hence still in the course as I have said before.

The 30th day the wind continued at WNW, very much wind; and about three or four of the clock in the afternoon, my Lord Admiral shot off a warning piece, and put out a flag of council; to the which myself, I was not able to go by reason of a hurt that I had received in my hip, by the reversing of one of our demi-cannons in the fight. But after the council was ended, my Lord Admiral sent aboard me a gentleman of his, both to see how I did, as also to tell me that my Lord Seymour had order to repair back again, to guard the Thames mouth from any attempt that might be made by the Duke of Parma; and that I was to attend upon him, and all the rest that were of his former charge; and that we should bear away in the twilight, as the enemy might not see our departing . . .

Written aboard the *Vanguard* in Harwich Road, at 7 of the clock at night.

Wynter

From Lord Henry Seymour, to Elizabeth I, 1 August 1588

The next day in the morning, and in council with his Lordship, it was resolved some exploit should be attempted the night following by fire, which was performed; and what distress came thereof we certainly know not, saving that the said put them from their anchoring, by means whereof one of their galleasses came athwart one of their own ships' hawses, whereby she broke her rudder, and constrained, for want of stirrege [steerage] to go into Calais Road, where certain of your hoys and pinnaces under my charge followed, and after long fight was by some of them boarded, slaying sundry Spaniards; the rest of them saved themselves by boat and swam into Calais, where they were received; the governor whereof shot at our men, enforcing them to forsake her, leaving thirty pieces of ordnance in her, as was supposed.

After this long fight, which continued almost six hours, and ended between 4 and 5 in the afternoon, until Tuesday at 7 in the evening, we continued by them, and your Majesty's fleet followed the Spaniards along the channel, until we came athwart the Brill, where I was commanded by my Lord Admiral, with your Majesty's fleet under my charge, to return back for the defence of your Majesty's coasts, if anything be attempted by the Duke of Parma; and therein have obeyed his Lordship much against my will, expecting your Majesty's further pleasure.

This, hoping God will confound all your enemies, and that shortly, do most humbly leave to trouble your most excellent Majesty. From aboard the *Rainbow*.

Your Majesty's most bounden and faithful fisherman,

Seymour

From Lord Henry Seymour, to Prince Maurice of Nassau, the Dutch Commander-in-Chief, 4 August 1588

To advertise you of our success since our meeting with the enemy and of the great fight on Monday, being 29 July, you should understand that the Spaniards have lost about eight great ships, of which one is a galleass, and by my estimation, there are slain of their men from five to six thousand. My Lord the Admiral of England continueth to follow them, keeping the advantage of the wind, and taking every occasion to fight with them. As for me, I have returned with our fleet, which will join you as soon as possible. Meanwhile I do not doubt that you will have an assured watch, so as the enemy cannot undertake anything to your hurt, the more as you can keep them closely shut up in Dunkirk until the wind and other occasions permit us to join our forces with yours. In my opinion, this will be much better. Thus commending myself to your good favour, I pray God to help us with his pity, and to give you, sir, a happy and long life. In haste . . .

[unsigned]

Her Majesty's Speech to the Troops at Tilbury, 9 August 1588

My loving people, we have been persuaded by some that are careful of our safety, to take heed how we commit ourselves to armed multi-tudes, for fear of treachery. But I assure you, I do not desire to live to distrust my faithful and loving people. Let tyrants fear. I have always so behaved myself that, under God, I have placed my chiefest strength and safeguard in the loyal hearts and good will of my subjects: and therefore I am come amongst you, as you see, at this time, not for my recreation and disport, but being resolved, in the midst and heat of the battle, to live or die amongst you all, to lay down for my God, and for my kingdom, and for my people, my honour and my blood, even in the dust. I know I have the body of a weak and feeble woman, but I have the heart and stomach of a king, and of a king of England too, and think foul scorn that Parma or Spain, or any prince of Europe should dare to invade the borders of my realm; to which, rather than any dishonour shall grow by me, I myself will take up arms, I myself will be your general, judge, and rewarder of every one of your virtues in the field. I know, already for your forwardness and you have deserved rewards and crowns; and we do assure you, in the word of a prince, they shall be duly paid you.

Deposition by Mathew Starke, seaman, 11 August 1588

Sir Martin Frobisher began some speeches as touching the service done in this action; who uttered these speeches following, saying: Sir Francis Drake reporteth that no man hath done any good service but he; but he shall well understand that others hath done as good service as he, and better too. He came bragging up at the first, indeed, and gave them his prow and his broadside; and then kept his lowfe [luff] and was glad that he was gone again, like a cowardly knave or traitor – I rest doubtful, but the one I will swear. Further, saith he, he hath done good service indeed, for he took Don Pedro. For after he had seen her in the evening, that she had spent her masts,

Queen Elizabeth I, at Tilbury: a panel at St. Faith's Church,
Gaywood.

The battle off Dunne Nose, Isle of Wight, on 25 July. The Spanish fleet is on the left, the English fleet on the right. Engraving from contemporary tapestry design.

The invincible Armada in combat with the English fleet. Engraving by Hogenberg.

then, like a coward, he kept by her all night, because he would have the spoil. He thinketh to cozen us of our shares of fifteen thousand ducats; but we will have our shares, or I will make him spend the best blood in his belly; for he hath had enough of those cozening cheats already.

Sir Francis was appointed to bear a light all that night; which light we looked for, but there was no light to be seen; and in the morning, when we should have dealt with them, there was not above five or six near unto the admiral, by reason we saw not his light.

From the Lord High Admiral, to the Privy Council, August 1588

The 19 July 1588, we had intelligence by one of the barks that his Lordship had left in the Sleeve for discovery, named the [*Golden Hind*] wherein was Captain Thomas Flemyng, that the fleet of Spain was seen near the Lizard, the wind being then southerly or south-west; and although the greater number of ships of the English army, being then in Plymouth, with that wind were very hard to be gotten out of harbour, yet the same was done with such diligence and good will, that many of them got abroad as though it had been with a fair wind. Whereupon, the 20th July, his Lordship, accompanied with 54 sail of his fleet, with that south-west wind plied out of the Sound; and being gotten out scarce so far as Idye Stone [Eddystone] the Spanish army was discovered, and were apparently seen of the whole fleet to the westwards as far as Fowey.

The next morning, being Sunday, 21 July 1588, all the English ships that were then come out of Plymouth had recovered the wind off Idye Stone, and about 9 of the clock in the morning, the Lord Admiral sent his pinnace, named the *Disdain*, to give the Duke of Medina defiance, and afterward in the *Ark* bare up with the admiral of the Spaniards wherein the Duke was supposed to be, and fought with her until she was rescued by divers ships of the Spanish army. In the meantime, Sir Francis Drake, Sir John Hawkins and Sir Martin Frobisher fought with the galleon of Portugal, wherein John Martinez de Recalde, vice-admiral, was supposed to be. The fight was so well maintained for the time that the enemy was constrained to give way and bear up room [to leeward] to the eastward, in which bearing up, a great galleon, wherein Don Pedro de Valdes was captain, became foul of another ship which spoiled and bare overboard his foremast and bolspreete [bowsprit] whereby he could not keep company with their fleet, but being with great dishonour left behind by the Duke, fell into our hands. There was also at that instant a great Biscayan, of 800 tons or thereabouts, that, by firing of a barrel of gunpowder, had her decks blown up, her stern blown out, and her steerage spoiled. This ship was for this night carried amongst the fleet by the galleasses.

The fight continued not above two hours; for the Lord Admiral, considering there were forty sail of his fleet as yet to come from Plymouth, thought good to stay their coming before he would hazard the rest too far, and therefore set out a flag of council, where his Lordship's considerate advice was much liked of, and order delivered unto each captain how to pursue the fleet of Spain; and so, dismissing each man to go aboard his own ship, his Lordship appointed Sir Francis Drake to set the watch that night.

This night the Spanish fleet bare alongst by the Start, and the next day, in the morning, they were as far to leeward as the Berry. Our own fleet, being disappointed of their light, by reason that Sir Francis Drake left the watch to pursue certain hulks which were descried very late in the evening, lingered behind not knowing whom to follow; only his Lordship, with the *Bear* and the *Mary Rose* in his company, somewhat in his stern, pursued the enemy all night within culverin shot; his own fleet being as far behind as, the next morning, the nearest might scarce be seen half mast high, and very many out of sight, which with a good sail recovered not his Lordship the next day before it was very late in the evening. This day, Sir Francis Drake with the *Revenge*, the *Roebuck* and a small bark or two in his company, took Don Pedro de Valdes, which was spoiled of his mast the day before; and having taken out Don Pedro and certain other gentlemen, sent away the same ship and company to Dartmouth, under the conduct of the *Roebuck*, and himself bare with the Lord Admiral, and recovered his Lordship that night, being Monday.

This Monday, being 22 July 1588, the Spaniards abandoned the ship that the day before was spoiled by fire, to the which his Lordship sent the Lord Thomas Howard and Sir John Hawkins, knight, who together, in a small skiff of the *Victory's*, went aboard her, where they saw a very pitiful sight – the deck of the ship fallen down, the steerage broken, the stern blown out, and about fifty poor creatures burnt with powder in most miserable sort. The stink in the ship was so unsavoury, and the sight within board so ugly, that the Lord Thomas Howard and Sir John Hawkins shortly departed and came unto the Lord Admiral to inform his Lordship in what case she was found; whereupon his Lordship took present order that a small bark named the Bark Flemyng [*Golden Hind*], wherein was Captain Thomas Flemyng, should conduct her to some port in England which he could best recover, which was performed, and the said ship brought into Weymouth the next day.

That night fell very calm, and the four galleasses singled them-selves out from their fleet, whereupon some doubt was had lest in the night they might have distressed some of our small ships which were short of our fleet, but their courage failed them, for they attempted nothing.

The next morning, being Tuesday, 23 July 1588, the wind sprang up at north-east, and then the Spaniards had the wind of the English army, which stood in the north-westward, towards the shore. So did the Spaniards also. But that course was not good for the English army to recover the wind of the Spaniards, and therefore they cast about to the eastwards; whereupon the Spaniards bare room, offering [to] board our ships. Upon which coming room there grew a great fight. The English ships stood fast and abode their coming, and the enemy, seeing us to abide them, and divers of our ships to stay for them, as the *Ark*, the *Nonpareil*, the *Elizabeth Jonas*, the *Victory*, etc., and divers other ships, they were content to fall astern of the *Non-pareil*, which was the sternmost ship.

In the meantime, the *Triumph*, with five ships, viz., the *Merchant Royal*, the *Centurion*, the *Margaret and John*, the *Mary Rose* and the *Golden Lion*, were so far to leeward and separated from our fleet, that the galleasses took courage and bare room with them and assaulted them sharply. But they were very well resisted by those ships for the space of an hour and a half. At length certain of her Majesty's ships bare with them, and then the galleasses forsook them. The wind then shifted to the south-eastwards and so to SSW, at what time a troop of her Majesty's ships and sundry merchants' assailed the Spanish fleet so sharply to the westward that they were all forced to give way and to bear room; which his Lordship perceived, together with the distress that the *Triumph* and the five merchant ships in her company were in, called unto certain of her Majesty's ships then near at hand

and charged them straitly to follow him, and to set freshly upon the Spaniards, and to go within musket shot of the enemy before they should discharge any one piece of ordnance, thereby to succour the *Triumph*; which was very well performed by the *Ark*, the *Elizabeth Jonas*, the Galleon of Leicester, the *Golden Lion*, the *Victory*, the *Mary Rose*, the *Dreadnought* and the *Swallow* – for so they went in order into the fight. Which the Duke of Medina perceiving, came out with sixteen of his best galleons, to impeach his Lordship and to stop him from assisting of the *Triumph*. At which assault, after wonderful sharp conflict, the Spaniards were forced to give way and to flock together like sheep. In this conflict one William Coxe, captain of a small pinnace of Sir William Wynter's, named the *Delight*, showed himself most valiant in the face of his enemies at the hottest of the encounter, where afterwards lost his life in the service with a great shot. Towards the evening, some four or five ships of the Spanish fleet edged out of the south-westwards, where some other of our ships met them, amongst which *Mayflower* of London discharged some pieces at them very valiantly, which ship and company at sundry other times behaved themselves stoutly.

This fight was very nobly continued from morning until evening, the Lord Admiral being always [in] the hottest of the encounter, and it may well be said that for the time there was never seen a more terrible value of great shot, nor more hot fight than this was; for although the musketeers and arquebusiers of crock [using rests for their weapons] were then infinite, yet could they not be discerned nor heard for that the great ordnance came so thick that a man would have judged it to have been a hot skirmish of small shot, being all the fight long within half musket shot of the enemy.

This great fight being ended, the next day, being Wednesday, 24 July 1588, there was little done, for that in the fight on Sunday and Tuesday much of our munition had been spent, and therefore the Lord Admiral sent divers barks and pinnaces unto the shore for a new supply of such provisions. This day the Lord Admiral divided his fleet into four squadrons, whereof he appointed the first to attend himself; the second his Lordship committed to the charge of Sir Francis Drake; the third to Sir John Hawkins, and the fourth to Sir Martin Frobisher. This afternoon his Lordship gave order that, in the night, six merchant ships out of every squadron should set upon the Spanish fleet in sundry places, at one instant, in the

night time, to keep the enemy waking; but all that night fell out to
be so calm that nothing could be done.

The next morning, being 25 July 1588, there was a great galleon
of the Spaniards short of her company to the southwards. They of
Sir John Hawkins his squadron, being next, towed and recovered
so near that the boats were beaten off with musket shot; whereupon
three of the galleasses and an armado issued out of the Spanish fleet,
with whom the Lord Admiral in the *Ark*, and the Lord Thomas
Howard in the *Golden Lion*, fought a long time and much damaged
them, that one of them was fain to be carried away upon the careen;
and another, by a shot from the *Ark*, lost her lantern, which came
swimming by, and the third his nose. There was many good shots
made by the *Ark* and *Lion* at the galleasses with their long boats. At
length it began to blow a little gale, and the Spanish fleet edged up
to succour their galleasses, and so rescued them and the galleon, after
which time the galleasses were never seen in fight any more, so bad
was their entertainment in this encounter. Then the fleets drawing
near one to another, there began some fight, but it continued not
long, saving that the *Nonpareil* and the *Mary Rose* struck their topsails and lay awhile by the whole fleet of Spain very bravely, during
which time the *Triumph*, to the northward of the Spanish fleet, was
so far to leeward as, doubting that some of the Spanish army might
weather her, she towed off with the help of sundry boats, and so
recovered the wind. The *Bear* and the *Elizabeth Jonas*, perceiving her
distress, bare with her for her rescue, and put themselves, through
their hardiness, into like perils, but made their parties good notwithstanding, until they had recovered the wind; and so that day's fight
ended, which was a very sharp fight for the time.

Now, forasmuch as our powder and shot was well wasted, the
Lord Admiral thought it was not good in policy to assail them any
more until their coming near unto Dover, where he should find the
army which he had left under the conduction of the Lord Henry
Seymour and Sir William Wynter, knight, ready to join with his
Lordship, whereby our fleet should be much strengthened, and in
the meantime, better store of munition might be provided from the
shore. On Friday, being 26 July 1588, his Lordship, as well in
reward of their good services in these former fights, as also for the
encouragement of the rest, called the Lord Thomas Howard, the
Lord Sheffield, Sir Roger Townshend, Sir Martin Frobisher and

Sir John Hawkins, and gave them all the order of knighthood aboard the *Ark*. All this day and Saturday, being 27 July, the Spaniards went always before the English army like sheep, during which time the justices of peace near the seacoast, the Earl of Sussex, Sir George Carey, and the captains of the forts and castles alongst the coast, sent us men, powder, shot, victuals and ships to aid and assist us. On Saturday, in the evening the Spanish fleet came near unto Calais on the coast of Picardy, and there suddenly came to an anchor over against betwixt Calais and Scales Cleeves [Calais Cliffs] and our English fleet anchored short of them within culverin shot of the enemy.

The Spaniards sent notice of their arrival presently unto the Duke of Parma, but by cause [because] there should be no time detracted to permit their forces to join, the Lord Admiral, 28 July 1588, about midnight, caused eight ships to be fired and let drive amongst the Spanish fleet; whereupon they were forced to let slip or cut cables at half and to set sail. By reason of which fire the chief galleass came foul of another ship's cable and brake her rudder, by means whereof he was forced the next day to row ashore near the haven's mouth and town of Calais; whereupon the Lord Admiral sent his long boat, under the charge of Amyas Preston, gentleman, his lieutenant, and with him Mr Thomas Gerrard and Mr [William] Harvey together with other gentlemen, his Lordship's followers and servants, who took her and had the spoil of her. There entered into her about 100 Englishmen. And for that she was aground and sewed two foot, and could not be gotten off, they left her to Monsr. Gourdan, Captain of Calais, where she lieth sunk.

Now that the Lord Henry Seymour and Sir William Wynter were joined with us, our fleet was near about 140 sail – of ships, barks and pinnaces etc., the Lord Admiral, Sir Francis Drake in the *Revenge*, accompanied with Mr Thomas Fenner in the *Nonpareil* and the rest of his squadron, set upon the fleet of Spain and gave them a sharp fight. And within short time, Sir John Hawkins in the *Victory*, accompanied with Mr Edward Fenton in the *Mary Rose*, Sir George Beeston in the *Dreadnought*, Mr Richard Hawkins in the *Swallow*, and the rest of the ships appointed to his squadron, bare with the midst of the Spanish army, and there continued hotly; and then came the Lord Admiral, the Lord Thomas Howard, the Lord Sheffield, near the place where the *Victory* had been before, where these noblemen did very valiantly. Astern of these was a great galleon assailed by the Earl of Cumberland and Mr George Ryman [Raymond] in the *Bonaventure* most worthily, and being also beaten with the Lord Henry Seymour in the *Rainbow*, and Sir William Wynter in the *Vanguard*, yet she recovered into the fleet. Notwithstanding, that night, she departed from the army and was sunk. After this, Mr Edward Fenton in the *Mary Rose* and a galleon encountered each other, the one standing to the eastward and the other to the westward, so close as they could conveniently one pass by another, wherein the captain and company did very well. Sir Robert Southwell that day did worthily behave himself, as he had done many times before; so did Mr Robert Crosse in the *Hope*, and most of the rest of the captains and gentlemen. This day did the Lord Henry Seymour and Sir William Wynter so batter two of the greatest armados that they were constrained to seek the coast of Flanders, and were afterwards, being distressed and spoiled, taken by the Zealanders and carried into Flushing. In this fight it is known that there came to their end sundry of the Spanish ships, besides many other unknown to us.

After this Monday's fight, which was 29 July 1588, the Lord Admiral on 30 July appointed the Lord Henry Seymour, Sir William Wynter and their fleet to return back again unto the Narrow Seas, to guard the coasts there, and himself, determining to follow the Spanish army with his fleet until they should come so far northward as the Frith in Scotland if they should bend themselves that way, thought good to forbear any more to assault them till he might see what they purposed to do, verily thinking that they would put into the Frith, where his Lordship had devised stratagems to make an end of them; but the Spaniards kept a course for the Isles of Scotland, and of purpose, to our seeming, to pass home that way, by the north of Scotland and west part of Ireland.

When we were coming into 55 degrees and 13 minutes to the northward, thirty leagues east of Newcastle, the Lord Admiral determined to fight with them again on the Friday, being 2 August, but by some advice and counsel his Lordship stayed that determination, partly because we saw their course and meaning was only to get away that way to the northward to save themselves, and partly also for that many of our fleet were unprovided of victuals; for our supply, which her Majesty had most carefully provided and caused to be in readiness, knew not where to seek for us. It was therefore concluded that we should leave the Spanish fleet and direct our course for the Frith in Scotland, as well for the refreshing of our victuals as also for the performing of some other business which the Lord Admiral thought convenient to be done; but the wind coming contrary – viz. westerly – the next day the Lord Admiral altered his course and returned back again for England with his whole army, whereof some recovered the Downs, some Harwich and some Yarmouth, about 7 August 1588.

[unsigned]

From the Lord High Admiral and others, to the Privy Council, 1 August 1588

We whose names are hereunder written have determined and agreed in Council to follow and pursue the Spanish fleet until we have cleared our own coast and brought the Frith west of us; and then to return back again, as well to revictual our ships, which stand in extreme scarcity, as also to guard and defend our own coast at home; with further protestation that, if our wants of victuals and munition were supplied, we would pursue them to the furthest that they durst have gone.

C. Howard	George Cumberland
T. Howard	Edmonde Sheffeylde
Fra. Drake	Edw. Hoby
John Hawkins	
Thomas Fenner	

2 August 1588

Determined by the Council to return from thwart of the Frith.

CHAPTER SIX
War: Defeat

*Los vientos eran contrarios, la luna estaba crecida,
los peces daban gemidos, por el mal tiempo que hacia.*

Romance del aviso de la Fortuna y de la derrota de don Rodrigo
(Old Spanish Ballad.)

(The winds were adverse and the moon was full, the fish uttered groans at that bad weather that arose.)

The governors of the Spanish colonies in Mexico, Peru and the Caribbean, when discussing Philip II's methods of government, used to say in jest: 'If death came from Madrid, we should all be immortal.' They were a long way from home; communications were carried by sailing ships with a maximum speed of six knots; and Philip was a most careful, hard-working correspondent. He had taken too much to heart the advice of his father, the Emperor Charles V, whom he greatly admired: 'Do everything yourself.' Even his charming and affectionate letters to his young children were models of the epistolary art. Ironically the commanders of his great enterprise were too near the palace-monastery of San Lorenzo, thirty miles from Madrid, where, apart from many hours spent kneeling in prayer before the altar of the magnificent chapel, he spent almost all his time at his desk. Such devotion to duty set an example followed by the greatest noblemen in the land. When therefore the Duke of Medina Sidonia realised, after the violent June storm encountered when the Armada first set sail, that the ships re-assembled at Corunna were sadly battered and his fighting men short of victuals and water, he could not on his own authority cancel the operation, though he was perfectly justified in saying that his forces had become much weaker than those of the enemy. Instead he had to refer to Madrid, and received the royal command to proceed. In like circum-stances, when the marshals of Napoleon's Grand Army, ordered to capture Moscow, had gone no further than Smolensk, they knew that they ought not to proceed, but their imperious master overruled them.

For the voyage to England the Duke had fair weather and a good wind, but off Plymouth his training and character prevented him from disregarding Philip's orders and going in to the attack, though there were with him a number

*of high-ranking officers of more fiery nature who would gladly have done so.
As he sailed up the Channel he could reasonably have expected a succession of
fast sailing boats from the Duke of Parma's headquarters bringing precise details of
his embarkation arrangements and marked charts showing where the Armada
should anchor. None came, and the fatal decision was made to wait in Calais Road.*

*The reports and dispatches that follow, describing each stage in the
campaign day by day, contain very few references to the difficulties outlined
above. They are written with professional objectivity, and, if Howard and
Drake had ever captured them, they would have found little with which to
disagree. The defeat of the Armada was not the fault of the sea commanders.*

Minutes of a meeting held at Corunna, 10/20 July 1588

On the royal galleon. The Duke submitted the question of the
advisability of the Armada leaving port, and begged each officer
present to give his opinion of the weather for the purpose. Don
Alonso de Leyva said that as the Duke had here the best sailors in
these parts, he should follow their advice. If they said he could sail,
even with difficulty, he ought to do so with all possible dilligence;
always on condition that nothing rash should be done which might
imperil the expedition. Diego Flores de Valdes said that the Duke
summoned them yesterday, and he, Flores, had said that today, the
20th, the weather would be worse, judging by appearances. As he
foretold, there has been a strong WNW wind blowing today, and a
heavy sea is running in. The evil appearances still continue, and fore-
bode very bad weather. As it is of so much importance that the Armada
should be kept intact, he is of opinion that it ought not to sail from this
port until the weather be fine and there be a clear north-west course.

Don Pedro de Valdes said that at yesterday's meeting he was of the
same opinion as Diego Flores, and neither yesterday nor today has
the weather been such that the Armada could safely weigh anchor
and leave port, as they had Cape Priorio to the north, which they
must double, and the wind must be more free for this to be done than
was required for the rest of the voyage. The Spanish ships of the
Armada might weather the point, as they were swift and could go
well to windward, but neither the hulks nor the Levanters could do
so without danger.

Captain Martín de Bertendona said that from yesterday until 11
o'clock today the weather had been excellent. He would not wish for

better weather for the sailing of the Armada; and the whole of the pilots and mariners with whom he had spoken were of the same opinion. Let the Duke, he said, inquire of them, and he would find it was so.

Don Diego Enriquez said the moon had come in with SW and W winds, and it had begun to wane with the same winds. It had blown from the SW today until 10 o'clock, and since then it had come from the W. If the wind settles in that quarter tomorrow, the Armada might sail.

Miguel de Oquendo confirmed the opinion of Diego Flores and Don Pedro de Valdes, for the same reasons as they gave, and also because the Armada is so close inshore, so that nine or ten leagues have to be traversed before they could get clear. If any cross wind were to come on in the interim, the Armada, or at least a considerable part of it, would run great risk.

Don Francisco de Bovadilla said that he was well aware that nothing was so important for his Majesty's service as the prompt sailing of the Armada, but in view of the difference of opinion that existed amongst the naval commanders and pilots, and because he, Bovadilla, was not a seaman, he could not advise the sailing of the fleet in such disturbed weather. He thought, however, that close watch should be kept, so that immediately the weather permitted they might sail without losing an hour.

Don Jorge Manriques said that he was not a sailor, but the season was already so advanced, and the summer so short, that he was of opinion that, as all great affairs must encounter some obstacles, the Armada should sail immediately it appeared possible to double Cape Priorio.

Juan Martinez de Recalde said it was quite clear that the old adage was true, 'Neither a bad sign in summer nor a good one in winter, but make the best of the opportunity that comes.' He was of opinion that if the weather tomorrow was similar to that of today, they should sail without waiting for new moons.

Medina Sidonia

From the Duke of Medina Sidonia, to Philip II, 20/30 July 1588

I wrote to your Majesty on the 23rd, that we were proceeding on our voyage in excellent weather. This continued all that day and the following days. No better weather could have been desired; and really if three or four of our ships had cared to clap on sail, even though they were not very swift, they might have arrived at the mouth of the Channel by Monday the 25th. But I, in this galleon, could only sail as fast as the scurviest ship in the fleet, as I have to wait for the slowest of them – verily some of them are dreadfully slow – so I was obliged, anxious as I was to get forward, thus to tarry on the way.

In sight of Cape Lizard, on board the galleon *San Martín*.

Medina Sidonia

From the Duke of Medina Sidonia, to Philip II, 11/21 August 1588

On 22 July 1588 the Duke and the whole of the Armada sailed from Corunna with a SW wind which continued for the next few days, the voyage being prosperous.

On the 25th the Duke sent Captain Don Rodrigo Tello to Dunkirk to advise the Duke of Parma of his coming, and to bring back intelligence of Parma's condition, and instructions with regard to the place where a junction of the forces should be effected.

On the 26th the weather was dead calm and overcast, which lasted until mid-day. The wind then went round to the N and the Armada sailed in an easterly direction until midnight, when the wind shifted to WNW, with heavy rain-squalls. The leading galley *Diana* was missed during this day. She was making so much water that the captain decided to run for a port.

On the 27th the same wind blew, but fresher, with very heavy sea. This lasted until midnight, and the storm caused a large number of ships and the other three galleys to separate from the Armada.

On Thursday, the 28th, the day broke clear and sunny, the wind and sea being more moderate. At dawn there were forty ships and the three galleys missing, whereupon the Duke ordered the lead to be cast and bottom was found at 75 fathoms, 75 leagues from the Scillys. The Duke then dispatched three pataches; one to the Lizard to see if the missing ships were there, and order them to await the Armada; another to reconnoitre the land; and a third to return on the course by which we have come to order the ships to make more sail, and bring up stragglers.

On Friday, the 29th, the Armada continued sailing with a westerly wind. The patache that went to the Lizard brought back news that our missing ships were ahead, under Don Pedro de Valdes, who had collected them and was awaiting the Armada.

During the afternoon all the ships, except Juan Martinez's flagship, with Maestre de Campo Nicolás de Isla on board, and the three galleys joined the Armada. The English coast was first sighted on this day. It was said to be Cape Lizard.

On the 30th, at dawn, the Armada was very near the shore. We were seen by the people on land, who made signal fires, and in the afternoon the Duke sent Ensign Juan Gil in a rowing boat to obtain intelligence. In the afternoon of the same day a number of ships were sighted, but as the weather was thick and rainy they could not be counted. Ensign Gil returned at night with four Englishmen in a boat, hailing, as they said, from Falmouth. They reported that they had seen the English fleet leave Plymouth that afternoon under the Lord Admiral of England and Drake.

On Sunday, the 31st, the day broke with the wind changed to the WNW in Plymouth Roads, and eighty ships were sighted to windward of us; and towards the coast to leeward eleven other ships were seen, including three large galleons which were cannonading some of our vessels. They gradually got to windward and joined their own fleet.

Our Armada placed itself in fighting order, the flagship hoisting the royal standard at the foremast. The enemy's fleet passed, cannonading our vanguard, which was under Don Alonso de Leyva, and then fell on to the rearguard commanded by Admiral Juan Martinez de Recalde. The latter, in order to keep his place and repel the attack, although he saw his rearguard was leaving him unsupported and joining the rest of the Armada, determined to await the fight. The enemy attacked him so fiercely with cannon that they crippled his rigging, breaking his stay, and striking his foremast twice with cannon balls. He was supported by the *Gran Grin*, a ship of the rearguard, and others. The royal flagship then struck her foresail, slackened her sheets, and lay to until Recalde joined the main squadron, when the enemy sheered off, and the Duke collected his fleet. This was all he was able to do, as the enemy had gained the wind, the English ships being swift and well handled, so that they could do as they liked with them. On the same afternoon Don Pedro de Valdes's flagship fouled the *Catalina*, one of the vessels of his squadron, the bowsprit and foresail of the flagship being broken. Don Pedro then joined the centre squadron of the Armada to repair the damage. Our Armada continued to manoeuvre until four o'clock in the afternoon, trying to gain the wind of the enemy. At this hour Oquendo's vice-flagship caught fire in the powder magazine, two of his decks and the poop castle being blown up. In this ship was the Paymaster-general of the Armada, with a part of his Majesty's treasure. When the Duke saw that the vessel was falling astern, he put about and went to her assistance, and gave a gun signal for the rest of the fleet to do likewise. He then ordered the pataches to go to the aid of Oquendo's ship. The fire was extinguished and the enemy, who was making for Oquendo's ship, put about when he saw the Duke's flagship standing by her. The ship was therefore recovered and was again incorporated with the Armada. During this manoeuvre the foremast of Don Pedro de Valdes's ship gave way at the hatches and fell on the mainsail boom. The Duke again put about to help him by sending him a hawser, but although great efforts were made, the wind and weather did not admit of this being done. Don Pedro's ship, therefore, began to be left astern, and, as it was now night, Diego Flores told the Duke that if he took in sail and stood by her the rest of the Armada would not perceive it, as most of the ships were far in advance, and he would find himself in the morning with less than half of the Armada. As we were so near the enemy's fleet he was of opinion that the Duke ought not to risk the whole of his force, as he was sure that if he stood by he would lose the day. In the face of this advice the Duke ordered Captain Ojeda to stand by Don Pedro's flagship [Nuestra Señora del Rosario] with four pataches, Don Pedro's vice-flagship [San Francisco], Diego Flores' flagship [San Cristóbal], and a galleass, to attempt to pass a hawser on board Don Pedro's ship and tow her, or else to take the men out of her. Neither of these things, however, was possible, in consequence of the heavy weather and rough sea, and its being night-time, and the Duke therefore proceeded on his voyage and joined his fleet, his intention being to keep the Armada well together, in view of what might happen next day. An attempt was made this night to tranship the burnt and wounded from Oquendo's vice-flagship [Nuestra Señora de la Rosa]. During the night the wind and sea rose considerably.

Monday, 1 August, the Duke ordered Don Alonso de Leyva to take the vanguard and join it to the rearguard, to form one body together with the three galleasses, and the galleons San Mateo, San Luis, Florenica and Santiago; making that squadron now consist of the forty-three best ships of the Armada, to withstand the enemy and prevent him from standing in the way of our junction with the Duke of Parma. The Duke, with the rest of the Armada, now formed the vanguard, the whole fleet being divided into two squadrons only. The rearguard was under the command of Don Alonso de Leyva, pending the repair of Juan Martinez's ship, the Duke in person commanding the vanguard. The Duke summoned the whole of the *sargentos mayores*, and ordered each one to go in a patache, and take his instructions round to every ship in the Armada, specifying in writing the position which they should respectively occupy. Orders were also given to them, in writing, to immediately hang any captain whose ship left her place, and they took with them the Provost Marshals and hangmen necessary for carrying out this order. Three *sargentos mayores* were told off for each of the two squadrons, whose duty it was to execute the aforesaid order.

At eleven o'clock on this day the captain of Oquendo's vice-flagship came and informed the Duke that the ship was foundering, and had been unmanageable. Orders were then given to tranship his Majesty's treasure, and the men on board, the ship afterwards to be sunk. In the afternoon of this day the Duke sent Ensign Juan Gil in a patache to inform the Duke of Parma of his position.

Tuesday, 2 August, broke fine, the enemy's fleet being to leeward, sailing towards the land, and making great efforts to gain the wind of us. The Duke also tacked towards the land and tried to keep the wind. He led, followed by the galleasses, the rest of the Armada being somewhat more distant, and the enemy noticing that the Duke's flagship was approaching the land, and that it was impossible to get to windward of her that way, put about to seaward and sailed on the opposite tack. Our ships, being to windward of the enemy, then attacked him. The enemy's flagship then turned tail and put her head seaward, and the following of our ships also attacked him and endeavoured to close with him, namely: the *San Marcos*, *San Luis*, *San Mateo*, *La Rata*, Oquendo, *San Felipe*, *San Juan de Sicilia* with Don Diego Tellez Enriquez on board (which ship had been near the enemy since morning), the galleon *Florencia*, the galleon *Santiago*, the galleon *San Juan*, with Don Diego Enriquez, son of the Viceroy of Peru, on board, and the Levant ship *Valencera*, with the Maestre de Campo, Don Alonso de Luzon, on board. The vanguard galleasses approached quite close to the enemy, thanks to the current, and the Duke sent them orders to make every effort to close – using both sail and oar. The Duke's flagship also turned to attack. The galleasses caught up with some boats of the enemy's having got quite close to the enemy for the purpose of boarding. But it was all useless, for when the enemy saw that our intention was to come to close quarters with him, he sheered off to seaward, his great advantage being in the swiftness of his ships. Soon afterwards the enemy's ships returned, with the wind and tide in their favour, and attacked Juan Martinez de Recalde in the rearguard. Don Alonso de Leyva reinforced the latter, and our flagship, which was then in the midst of the main squadron, sailed to the support of the ships of the Armada which were mixed up with the enemy's rearguard and separated from the mass of both fleets. The Duke ordered Captain Marolín to go in a feluca and try to guide the vessels which were near the Duke's flagship to the support of Juan Martinez de Recalde. When this was effected the enemy left Juan Martinez, and attacked the Duke's flagship, which was isolated and on her way to the assistance of the said ships. When our flagship saw that the flagship of the enemy was leading towards her, she lowered her topsails, and the enemy's flagship passed her followed by the whole of his fleet, each ship firing at our flagship as it passed. The guns on our flagship were served well and rapidly, and by the time half of the enemy's fleet had passed her the fire became more distant. The flagship was reinforced by Juan Martinez de Recalde, Don Alonso de Leyva, the Marqués de Penafiel, in the *San Marcos*, and Oquendo, although by the time they came up the hottest fury was passed. The enemy then put about to seaward. We watched the enemy's flagship retreating and she appeared to have suffered some damage. The enemy's vessels that were engaged with our vanguard were also withdrawn. One of the most forward of our ships in this three hours' skirmish was the galleon *Florencia*.

Wednesday, the 3rd, Juan Martinez de Recalde again assumed command of the rearguard, Don Alonso de Leyva remaining with him, the forty odd ships that formed the rearguard being divided between them. At dawn the enemy was near our rear, the vice-flagship receiving some cannon fire from him. Our galleasses fired their stern guns, Juan Martinez's, Don Alonso de Leyva's, and the rest of the ships of the rear squadron did likewise without leaving their positions, and the enemy then retired without attempting anything further; our galleasses having disabled the rigging of the enemy's flagship, and brought down his mainsail boom.

Portrait of El Greco of a man thought to be Don Alonso de Leyva, drowned in the wreck of the Girona.

Alexander Farnese, the Duke of Parma.

Thursday, the 4th, St Dominic's day, the hulk *St Ana* and a galleon of Portugal had fallen somewhat astern, and were fiercely attacked by the enemy. The galleasses, Don Alonso de Leyva's and other ships came to their assistance. Although the two ships were surrounded by many enemies the galleasses were successful in bring, ing them out. Whilst the skirmish was going on in the rear, the enemy's flagship, with other large vessels, fell upon our royal flagship which was leading the vanguard. They came closer than on the previous day, firing off their heaviest guns from the lowest deck, cutting the trice of our mainmast, and killing some of our soldiers. The *San Luis*, with the Maestre de Campo Don Agustín [Mexia] on board, came to the rescue, and the enemy was also faced by Juan Martinez de Recalde, the *San Juan* of Diego Flores' squadron, with Don Diego Enriquez on board, and Oquendo, who placed himself before our flagship, as the current made it impossible for him to stand alongside. Other vessels did likewise, although the enemy retired. The enemy's flagship had suffered considerable damage, and had drifted somewhat to leeward of our Armada. Our flagship then turned upon her, supported by Juan Martinez de Recalde, the *San Juan de Sicilia*, the flagship of the galleons of Castile, the *Gran Grin* and the rest of our ships. To windward of us was the enemy's fleet coming up to support their flagship, which was in such straits that she had to be towed out by eleven long boats, lowering her standard and firing guns for aid. Our royal flagship and vice-flagship in the meanwhile were approaching so close in to her that the rest of the enemy's vessels gave signs of coming in to her assistance, and we made sure that at last we should be able to close with them, which was our only way of gaining the victory. At this moment the wind freshened in favour of the enemy's flagship, and we saw she was getting away from us, and had no further need of the shallops that were towing her out. The enemy was then able to get to windward of us again. As the Duke saw that further attack was useless, and that we were already off the Wight, he fired a signal gun and proceeded on the voyage, followed by the rest of the Armada in good order; the enemy remaining a long way astern. On this day the Duke sent Captain Pedro de León to Dunkirk to advise the Duke of Parma as to his whereabouts and inform him of events, pressing him to come out with all possible speed and join the Armada. Don Diego Enriquez, son of the Viceroy, was placed in command of Don

Pedro de Valdes's squadron, as he had shown great care in the science of seamanship.

Friday, the 5th, broke calm, both fleets being within sight of each other, and the Duke sent another feluca to the Duke of Parma with the pilot Domingo Ochoa on board, to beg him to send us some cannon balls of 4, 5 and 10 lbs as a great many had been spent in the skirmishing of the last few days. He was also instructed to request Parma to send out forty flyboats immediately to join the Armada; and so by their aid to enable us to come to close quarters with the enemy, which we had hitherto found it quite impossible to do, in consequence of our vessels being very heavy in comparison with the lightness of the enemy's ships. Ochoa was also instructed to press upon the Duke of Parma the necessity of his being ready to come out and join the Armada the very day it appeared in sight of Dunkirk. The Duke was very anxious on this point, as he feared Parma was not at Dunkirk; Don Rodrigo Tello not having returned, and no messenger having come from Parma. At sunset a breeze sprang up and the Armada again got under way on the voyage towards Calais.

At daybreak on Saturday, 6th, the fleets were close together, and sailed on without exchanging shots until ten o'clock in the day, our Armada having the wind astern and the rearguard well up, in good order. At this hour the coast of France was sighted near Boulogne and we proceeded on our voyage to Calais Roads, where we arrived at four o'clock in the afternoon. There was some difference of opinion as to whether we should anchor here, the majority being in favour of sailing on. The Duke, however, was informed by his pilots that if he proceeded any further the currents would force him to run out of the Channel into Norwegian waters, and he consequently decided to anchor off Calais, seven leagues from Dunkirk, where Parma might join him. At five o'clock the order to drop anchor was given to the whole Armada, and Captain Heredia was sent to visit the governor of Calais, M. de Gourdan, to explain the reason why we had anchored there and offer him friendship.

This afternoon the enemy's fleet was reinforced by thirty-six sail, including five great galleons. This was understood to be John Hawkins' squadron, which had been watching Dunkirk, and the whole of the English fleet now anchored a league distant from our Armada. Captain Heredia returned that night from Calais, bringing friendly assurances and promises of service from the governor. The

Duke dispatched Secretary Arceo to Parma, to inform him of the position of the Armada, and to say that it was impossible for it to remain where it was without very great risk.

On Sunday, the 7th, at daybreak, Captain Don Rodrigo Tello arrived from Dunkirk and reported that the Duke of Parma was at Bruges, where he had visited him, and although he had expressed great joy at the arrival of the Armada, he had not come to Dunkirk up to the night of Saturday, the 6th, when Tello had left there, nor had the embarcation of the men and stores been commenced.

On Sunday morning the governor of Calais sent his nephew to visit the Duke bringing with him a great present of fresh provisions. He informed the Duke that the place where he was lying was extremely dangerous to stay in, in consequence of the cross currents of the Channel being very strong. In view of the friendly attitude of the governor, the Duke sent the Provedore Bernage de Pedroso, with the paymaster, to purchase victuals. He also sent at night Don Jorge Manrique to Parma, to urge upon him to expedite his coming out.

At midnight two fires were perceived on the English fleet, and these two gradually increased to eight. They were eight vessels with sails set, which were drifting with the current directly towards our flagship and the rest of the Armada, all of them burning with great fury. When the Duke saw them approaching, and that our men had not diverted them, he, fearing that they might contain fire machines or mines, ordered the flagship to let go the cables, the rest of the Armada receiving similar orders, with an intimation that when the fires had passed they were to return to the same positions again. The leading galleass in trying to avoid a ship ran foul of the *San Juan de Sicilia*, and became so crippled that she was obliged to drift ashore. The current was so strong that although the flagship, and some of the vessels near her, came to anchor again and fired off a signal gun, the other ships of the Armada did not perceive it, and were carried by the current towards Dunkirk.

At dawn on Monday, the 8th, the Duke seeing that his Armada was far ahead, and that the enemy was bearing down upon us with all sail, weighed his anchor to go and collect the Armada, and endeavour to bring it back to its previous position. The wind freshened from the NW, which is on to the shore, and the English fleet of 136 sail, with the wind and tide in its favour, was overhauling us with great speed, whereupon the Duke recognised that if he con⁄

tinued to bear room and tried to come up with the Armada all would be lost, as his Flemish pilots told him he was already very near the Dunkirk shoals. In order to save his ships he accordingly determined to face the whole of the enemy's fleet, sending pataches to advise the rest of the Armada to luff close, as they were running on to the Dunkirk shoals. The enemy's flagship, supported by most of his fleet, attacked our flagship with great fury at daybreak, approaching within musket-shot and sometimes within arquebus-shot. The attack lasted until three in the afternoon, without a moment's cessation of the artillery fire, nor did our flagship stand away until she had extricated the Armada from the sandbanks. The galleon San Marcos, with the Marqués de Penafiel on board, stood by the flagship the whole time. The leading galleass, being unable to follow the Armada, ran aground at the mouth of Calais harbour, followed by some of the enemy's vessels. It is believed that she was succoured by the guns of the fortress of Calais, and that the men on board of her were saved. Don Alonso de Leyva, Juan Martinez de Recalde, Oquendo's flagship, the whole of the ships of the Castilian and Portuguese Maestros de Campo, Diego Flores' flagship, Bertendona's flagship, the galleon San Juan of Diego Flores, with Don Diego Enriquez on board, and the San Juan de Sicilia with Don Diego Tellez Enriquez on board, withstood the enemy's attack as well as they could, and all of these ships were so much damaged as to be almost unable to offer further resistance, most of them not having a round of shot more to fire. Don Francisco de Toledo, who brought up the rear, attempted to close with the enemy. The latter turned upon him with so hot an artillery fire that he was in difficulty. Don Diego de Pimentel then came to his support, but they were both of them being overpowered, when Juan Martinez de Recalde, with Don Agustín Mexia, bore up and extricated them. But, notwithstanding this, these two ships once more got in the midst of the enemy, together with Don Alonso de Luzón's ship, the Santa María de Begona, with Garibay on board, and the San Juan de Sicilia, with Don Diego Tellez Enriquez on board. They very nearly closed with the enemy without grappling, the English keeping up an artillery fire, from which our men defended themselves with musketry and arquebus fire, as they were so near. The Duke heard the sound of small arms, but was unable to distinguish what was going on from the maintop, in consequence of the smoke; but he saw that two of our ships were amongst the enemy, and that the latter, leaving our flagship, concentrated all his fleet in that direction, so the Duke ordered the flagship to put about to assist them. The Duke's ship was so much damaged with cannon-shot between wind and water that the inflow could not be stopped, and her rigging was almost cut to shreds, but nevertheless, when the enemy saw that she was approaching, his ships left the vessels they were attacking, namely, those of Don Alonso de Luzón, Garibay, Don Francisco de Toledo, Don Diego Pimentel, and Don Diego Tellez Enriquez. The three latter were most exposed, and were completely crippled and unserviceable, nearly all the men on board being either killed or wounded, although that of Don Diego Tellez Enriquez made shift to follow us in very bad case. The Duke then collected his force, and the enemy did likewise. The Duke ordered pataches to be sent and take off the men from the *San Felipe*, and the *San Mateo*, but Don Diego Pimentál refused to abandon the ship, sending Don Rodrigo Vivero and Don Luis Vanegas to the Duke to ask him to send someone on board to inspect the vessel, and ascertain whether she was seaworthy. The Duke sent a pilot and a diver from this galleon, although we were in great risk without him. As the night was falling and the sea was very heavy they were unable to reach the *San Mateo*, but they saw it that night at a distance, falling off towards Zeeland. The galleon *San Felipe* went alongside the hulk *Doncella*, and transhipped on board of the latter all the company. But when Don Francisco had gone on board the hulk a cry was raised that she was foundering, and Captain Juan Poza de Santiso leapt on to the *San Felipe* again, followed by Don Francisco. This was a great misfortune, for it was not true that the hulk was sinking, and the *San Felipe* also went towards Zeeland with Don Francisco on board, after the Duke had been informed that he and all his men were safe on the hulk. The sea was so heavy that nothing else could be done, and it was even impossible to patch up the injuries to the flagship; whereby she was in great danger of being lost. The Duke wished during this day to turn and attack the enemy with the whole Armada, in order to avoid running out of the Channel, but the pilots told him it was impossible, as both wind and tide were against us; the wind blowing from the NW towards the land. They said that he would be forced either to run up into the North Sea, or wreck all the Armada on the shoals. He was therefore utterly unable to avoid going out of the Channel, nearly all of our trustworthy ships being so damaged as to be unfit to resist attack, both on account of the cannon fire to which they had been exposed, and their own lack of projectiles.

Tuesday, the 9th, eve of St Lorenzo. At two o'clock in the morning the wind blew so strongly that, although our flagship was brought up as close to the wind as possible, she began to fall off to leeward towards the Zeeland coast, the Duke's intention having been to stay so that he might again enter the Channel. At daybreak the NW wind fell somewhat, and we discovered the enemy's fleet of 109 ships rather over half a league astern of us. Our flagship remained in the rear with Juan Martinez de Recalde, Don Alonso de Leyva, the galleasses, and the galleon *San Marcos* and *San Juan* of Diego Flores the rest of the Armada being distant and a great deal to leeward. The enemy's ships bore down on our flagship, which came round to the wind and lay to; the galleasses placed themselves in front, and the rest of our rearguard stood by ready to repel attack, whereupon the enemy retired. The Duke then fired two guns to collect the Armada and sent a pilot in a patache to order the ships to keep their heads close to the wind, and they were almost on the Zeeland shoals. This prevented the enemy from approaching closer to us, as they saw that our Armada was going to be lost; indeed the experienced pilots who accompanied the Duke assured him at this time that it was impossible to save a single ship of the Armada, as they must inevitably be driven by the north-west wind on to the banks of Zeeland. God alone could rescue them. From this desperate peril, in only six and a half fathoms of water, we were saved by the wind shifting by God's mercy to the SW, and the Armada was then able to steer a northerly course without danger to any of our ships. The orders sent by the Duke in the pataches were that the whole of the ships were to follow in the wake of the flagship, as otherwise they would run upon the banks. The same afternoon the Duke summoned the generals and Don Alonso de Leyva to decide what should be done. The Duke submitted the state of the Armada, and the lack of projectiles, a fresh supply of which had been requested by all the principal ships; and asked the opinion of those present as to whether it would be best to return to the English Channel, or sail home to Spain by the North Sea, the Duke of Parma not having sent advice that he would be able to come out promptly. The council unanimously resolved in favour of returning to the Channel if the weather would allow of it, but if not, then that they should obey the wind and sail to Spain by the North Sea, bearing in mind that the Armada was lacking all things necessary, and that the ships that had hitherto resisted were badly crippled. The wind from the SSW kept increasing in violence, and the Duke continued to get further out to sea, followed by the whole of the enemy's fleet. With regard to the fighting on the flagship, taking up of position, etc., the Duke followed the advice of the Maestre de Campo, Don Francisco de Bobadilla, who had many years' experience of fighting on land and sea. He had been ordered by the Duke at Corunna to leave the galleon *San Marcos* and go aboard the flagship, and had left on the *San Marcos* the Marqués de Peñafiel, who declined to go to the flagship in consequence of the gentlemen who were with him on the former galleon. In the management of the Armada, and in maritime matters, the Duke was guided by General Diego Flores, who had also been ordered to go on board the flagship, he being one of the oldest and most experienced of seamen.

On Wednesday, the 10th, the Armada was under way with a fresh SW wind and a heavy sea, the enemy's fleet following us. In the afternoon the violence of the wind abated, and the enemy came under full sail towards our rearguard. The Duke, seeing this, and that the rearguard under Juan Martinez de Recalde was weak in ships, struck his topsails and awaited the rearguard; at the same time fired the signal of three guns at intervals, to order the rest of the Armada, which was under full sail, to shorten sail and stand by for the rearguard and the flagship. What was done in these circumstances by our Armada will be related by Don Baltasar de Zuñiga. When the enemy saw that our flagship, the galleasses, and twelve of our best ships were standing by, he shortened sail and dropped astern without firing at us. John Hawkins with his squadron turned back during the night.

On Friday, the 12th, at dawn, the enemy's fleet was quite close to us, but as they saw we were well together, and that the rearguard had been reinforced, the enemy fell astern and sailed towards England until we lost sight of him. Since then we have continued sailing with the same wind until we left the Norwegian Channel, and it has been impossible for us to return to the English Channel even if we desired to do so. We have now, the 20th August, doubled the last of the Scottish Islands to the north, and we have set our course with a NE wind for Spain.

Medina Sidonia

CHAPTER SEVEN

Spoils of War: Rejoicing

If you have victory, let the trumpet sound
For him that brought it.

King Lear V i 4v

For three weeks after Howard's return to port, neither Elizabeth nor Philip had any trustworthy news of the Armada. Drake shared the general opinion that Parma was a great soldier and would react 'as a bear robbed of her whelps'. Elizabeth delivered her famous speech to the troops at Tilbury on 8 August, when, without the knowledge of those present, the danger had passed. Walsingham was in her company. Burghley visited the camp a few days later. Though in his sixty-eighth year and in continuous bodily pain, he, like Walsingham and Leicester, had worked incessantly during the spring and summer. His amazing vitality was to carry him through another nine years of war-time service. Leicester on the other hand was worn out. He came to London in August, but on the 29th left for Buxton in Derbyshire, where he died on 4 September. On the journey he wrote to the Queen wishing her good health and long life. To his note she attached a slip of paper with the words 'His last letter', and put it in a little casket that she kept at her bedside, where it was found after her death. The anniversary of her accession, 11 November, celebrated in most years with a tournament, feastings and music, was marked with a great procession through the streets of London and a service of thanksgiving in old St Paul's.

Burghley seized the first possible moment to order the dismissal of both soldiers and sailors. Nothing that Howard, Leicester, Seymour or Hawkins could say persuaded him to part with a penny for wages due, once the Privy Council had heard that the danger was over. The commanders were apparently expected to find the money themselves. The sailors waited in vain for their pay, weak from exposure in the continuing cold and wet, and racked by fever after living for weeks in close quarters without proper sanitation or change of clothing. The weather was so bad that food could not be taken out to the ships at anchor, except with great difficulty.

Considerable care was taken of prisoners held in London and in Devon, though the feeding of them was a heavy local charge. Negotiations for the ransom of Don Pedro de Valdes and some high-ranking officers of his company took many months. He showed a fitting concern for the men from his estates who had been taken with him. There was comparatively little plunder, but even fine clothing was valued and sold. In Ireland, as usual, the accepted laws of war did not apply, and no prisoners were taken.

Minutes of the Privy Council, 27 July 1588. To Sir John Gilbert

Whereas in the Spanish ship lately taken on the seas and brought on that coast there were divers Spaniards, as well gentlemen soldiers as seafaring men, amounting in all to a great number, their Lordships thought good to require him by the examining of the said prisoners by such discreet means as he should think fittest to learn the qualities of the said persons and callings, and of what nations they were, that those of name and quality might be discerned and known from the rest and bestowed in safe prisons; the rest of baser sort to be distributed into such prisons as he should think fittest for their safe keeping, or else keep aboard the ships wherein they were taken, with some spare and reasonable diet out of their own provisions that remained in the ship, until further direction; and for the English men that were found amongst them, their Lordships had taken present order that already they should forthwith be sent up hither to the Court under sure safe-guard with as convenient speed as might be used.

From Sir John Hawkins, to Sir Francis Walsingham, 31 July 1588

The men have been long unpaid and need relief. I pray your Lordship that the money that should have gone to Plymouth may now be sent to Dover. August now cometh in, and this coast will spend ground tackle, cordage, canvas and victuals; all which would be sent to Dover in good plenty. With these things, and God's blessing, our kingdom may be preserved; which being neglected, great hazard may come. I write to your Lordship briefly and plainly. Your wisdom and experience is great; but this is a matter far passing all that hath been seen in our time or long before. And so praying to God for a happy deliverance from the malicious and dangerous practice of our enemies, I humbly take my leave. From the sea, aboard the *Victory*.

The Spaniards take their course for Scotland; my Lord doth follow them. I doubt not with God's favour, but we shall impeach their landing. There must be order for victual and money, powder and shot, to be sent after us.

Hawkins

Examination of Prisoners, 2 August 1588

Summary of interrogation at Bridewell of prisoners taken in the *Nuestra Señora del Rosario* of Ribadeo, Galicia, of 1,150 tons. Vincente Alvarez, captain.

Whether the intention of the fleet was to invade and conquer England or no; and who should have had the principal charge of that enterprise?

They were specially directed unto the Duke of Parma, who by the general report was the man that should take upon him the conquest of England; and that the Duke of Medina Sidonia had order to deliver his forces over unto the Duke of Parma, and to follow his directions in all things.

What they have heard or know of any help or succour that they should receive upon their landing in England?

It was commonly bruited amongst them that a third part or one half of the realm of England would join to their aid so soon as they should enter on the land.

What treasure was taken in the ship wherein they were taken?

There was in the ship wherein he was taken a chest of the King's, wherein there was 52,000 ducats, of which chest Don Pedro de Valdes had one key, and the King's Treasurer, or the Duke, another; besides 4,000 reals of this examinant's, and many other of the gentlemen had good store of money aboard the said ship. Also there was wrought plate of the Duke's and Don Pedro, but to what value he knoweth not; and that there was great store of precious jewels and rich apparel; and thinketh there was not four ships so rich in the whole armada...

Gregorio de Sotomayor:

I declare that King Philip did command that the fleet should be victualled for six months, but Luis Hezar and Francisco Duarte of Cadiz did victual them but for four months, and with that which was nought and rotten. For which occasion the King commanded them to be apprehended; and so they remained prisoners in Portugal at our coming away. And this is the very truth.

Note of plunder taken by Captain Cely from the Spanish prisoners in Bridewell ...

Of Alonso de la Serna:

> a coloured cloak, with a gold lace round about it; a pair of breeches of cloth of gold, a jerkin, embroidered with flowers, and laid over with a gold lace ...

Of the Ensign Bearer Bermudo:

> a cloak mandillion [mantle]; breeches of rash, laid over all with gold lace; and a blue stitched taffety hat, with a silver band and a plume of feathers.

Of Santiago:

> a pair of black velvet breeches.

Of Mateo de Fries:

> a pair of black satin breeches.

Minutes of the Privy Council, 5 August 1588.

To the Earl of Leicester, Lieutenant General of all her Majestys forces prepared against foreign invasion

The Queen's Majesty considering the great unseasonableness of the weather, and how, by reason of their service in the camp under his Lordship's charge, many of her good subjects are withdrawn from gathering in their harvest, to their great hinderance, hath entered this morning into consultation with their Lordships in what sort both they might be relieved and also her charges abridged, which, seeing (God be thanked) there is no apparent danger from the enemy, it is thought may be conveniently done at this time; for which purpose this bearer, Sir Thomas Sherley, is sent unto his Lordship to the intent his Lordship might consider thereof, and if he shall see no sufficient cause to the contrary, he may dismiss so many of the troops of the counties which are next adjoining as his Lordship shall think may be best spared, so as if any occasion of service should hereafter fall out, they may be in readiness to return upon any warning, and at their departure their Lordships think it convenient that his Lordship should cause them to be paid from the day that they entered into pay until the day of their dismission ...

From the Lord High Admiral, to Sir Francis Walsingham, 7 August 1588

In our last fight with the enemy before Gravelines, 29 July, we sank three of their ships, and made four to go room with the shore so leak as they were not able to live at sea. After that fight, notwithstanding that our powder and shot was well near all spent, we set on a brag countenance and gave them chase, as though we had wanted nothing, until we had cleared our own coast and some part of Scotland of them. And then, as well to refresh our ships with victuals, whereof most stood in wonderful need, as also in respect of our want of powder and shot, we made for the Frith, and sent certain pinnaces to dog the fleet until they should be past the Isles of Scotland, which I verily do believe they are left at their sterns ere this. We are persuaded that either they are past about Ireland, and so do what they can to recover their own coast, or else that they are gone for some part of Denmark. I have herewith sent unto your Honour a brief abstract of such accidents as have happened, which hereafter, at better leisure, I will explain by more particular relations.

    From aboard the *Ark*,
      Your very loving friend,

                                     Howard

Good Mr Secretary, let not her Majesty be too hasty in dissolving her force by sea and land ...

From Sir Francis Drake, to Elizabeth I, 8 August 1588

The absence of my Lord Admiral, most gracious sovereign, hath emboldened me to put my pen to the paper. On Friday last upon consideration, we cast the army of Spain so far to the northwards, as they could neither recover England nor Scotland; and within three days after, we were entertained with a great storm considering the time of year.

    If the wind hinders it not, I think they are forced to Denmark, and that for divers causes. Certain it is, that many of their people were sick and not a few killed; their ships, sails, ropes and waste, needeth great reparations, for that they had all felt of your Majesty's forces. If your Majesty thought it meet, it were not amiss you sent presently to

Denmark, to understand the truth, and to deal with that King accord⁄ing to your Majesty's great wisdom. I have not written this whereby your Majesty should diminish any of your forces. Your Highness's enemies are many; yet God hath and will hear your Majesty's prayers, putting your hand to the plough for the defence of his truth, as your Majesty hath begun. God, for his truth's sake, bless your sacred Majesty now and ever.

Written aboard your Majesty's good ship the *Revenge*.

Your Majesty's faithful vassal,

Drake

From Christian Huygens, Secretary to the State Council of the Dutch Republic, to the Privy Council, 8 August 1588

We praise and glorify God exceedingly for that it hath pleased him at divers times to give good success to her Majesty's navy against the common enemy; and we are glad that her Majesty hath favourably considered of the service that hath been done by us. It were greatly to be desired that we could have seconded her with stronger forces than we have here at this time, thereby to render the victory more perfect. But the misfortunes which have befallen this State, from the extra⁄ordinary and unheard of mutinies excited amongst our soldiers, have deprived us of the means whereby these countries could have armed greater forces by sea, so as better to have testified our zeal for the service of her Majesty.

On the other hand, your Lordships will also see how sure and certain it is that the Duke of Parma, understanding of the ill success of his enterprise against England, will, in his fury, turn the great power that he has brought together in Flanders against this country, to revenge himself, if it may be, for the loss and shame his master and he have had at the sea. We beseech your Lordships to take order that the forces of her Majesty in these parts shall be sufficient in number and in quality, as well of footmen as of horsemen, whereof, at this present, there is great lack; and, meantime, to continue your favours to this afflicted country in the great need that now is; assuring your Lordships that, on our part, we shall not fail to do to the uttermost of our ability for the service of her Majesty and for our own safety.

From the Hague,

Christian Huygens

From William Cecil, Lord Burghley, to Sir Francis Walsingham, 9 August 1588

I am not of opinion that the Spanish fleet will suddenly return from the north or the east, being weakened as they are, and knowing that our navy is returned to our coast, where they may repair their lacks, and be as strong as they were afore. And without a north or east wind the Spanish fleet cannot come back to England. I wish if they pass about Ireland, that four good ships, well manned and conducted, might distress a great number of them, being weather-beaten, and where the numbers of the gallants will not continue on shipboard.

As I perceive, the powder that was sent from Dover never came to my Lord Admiral. It is in vain to write any more for advice until, from my Lord Cobham, we may learn something of the Duke of Parma, who now resteth the enemy to be withstood.

At Tilbury or Gravesend.
Yours assured,

Burghley

From the Lord High Admiral, to Sir Francis Walsingham, 9 August 1588

After I had spoken with Mr Quarles at Sandwich, I galloped hither to the Commissioners, to understand by them of the state of the Duke of Parma . . .

Sir, I do hear that Colonel Morgan is come to Margate with 800 soldiers, and I do hear it should be for our ships. If it should be so, we must have victuals provided for them before we can receive them; for the victuals that Mr Quarles hath provided will not serve our company above three weeks; for the proportions is but for 7,600 men, and we are near 10,000. There must be care taken for it . . .

There is a number of poor men of the coast towns – I mean the mariners – that cry out for money, and they know not where to be paid. I have given them my word and honour that either the towns shall pay them, or I will see them paid. If I had not done so, they had run away from Plymouth by thousands. I hope there will be care had of it. Sir, money had need to come down for our whole company. Sir, I am going to Margate. In haste, fare ye well.

From Canterbury,
Your loving friend,

Howard

From Sir Francis Drake, to Sir Francis Walsingham, 10 August 1588

The Prince of Parma, I take him to be as a bear robbed of her whelps; and no doubt, but being so great soldier as he is, that he will presently, if he may, undertake some great matter, for his rest will stand now thereupon. It is for certain, that the Duke of Sidonia standeth somewhat jealous of him, and the Spaniards begin to hate him, their honour being touched so near, and many of their lives spent. I assure your Honour not so little as five thousand men less, than when we first saw them near Plymouth; divers of their ships sunk and taken; and they have nothing to say for themselves in excuse, but that they came to the place appointed, which was at Calais, and there staid the Duke of Parma's coming above twenty-four hours, yea, and until they were fired out. So this is my poor conclusion, if we may recover near Dunkirk this night, or tomorrow morning, so as their power may see us returned from the Channel, and ready to encounter them, if they once sally, that the next news you shall hear, will be the one to meeting against the other; which when it shall come to pass, or whether they meeting or no, let us all with one consent, both high and low, magnify and praise our most gracious and merciful God, for his infinite and unspeakable good-ness towards us.

Written with much haste, for that we are ready to set sail to prevent the Duke of Parma, this southerly wind, if it please God; for, truly, my poor opinion is, that we should have a great eye upon him.

Drake

PS Since the writing hereof, I have spoken with an Englishman, which came from Dunkirk yesterday; who saith, upon his life, there is no fear of the fleet. Yet would I willingly see it.

Drake

From Lord Henry Seymour, to Sir Francis Walsingham, 14 August 1588

Having had further conference with one of the Flushingers sent unto me from his admiral, I do send you likewise the admiral's letter itself, which I pray you to return, both that and others, after you have taken your pleasure. I perceive by him, likewise, they take a special care to send out fifty sails of North Hollanders in the pursuit of the Spaniards, for the better guarding of their coasts; and have restrained their fishermen that go for herrings, so as yet they will not suffer them to go to sea in these affairs although the state of the country dependeth upon that fishing. And even so, do commit you to God. From aboard the *Rainbow*.

Your assured friend to command,

Seymour

From Lord Henry Seymour, to Sir Francis Walsingham, 19 August 1588

Our men fall sick, by reason of the cold nights and cold mornings we find; and I fear me they will drop away far faster than they did the last year with Sir Henry Palmer, which was thick enough.

From aboard the *Rainbow*.

Seymour

From the Lord High Admiral, to Elizabeth I, 22 August 1588

My most gracious Lady, with great grief I must write unto you in what state I find your fleet. The infection is grown very great and in many ships, and now very dangerous; and those that come in fresh are soonest infected; they sicken the one day and die the next. It is a thing that ever followeth such great services, and I doubt not but with good care and God's goodness, which doth always bless your Majesty and yours, it will quench again.

Howard

From the Lord High Admiral, to the Privy Council, 22 August 1588

As I left some of the ships infected at my coming up, so I do find, by their reports that have looked deeply into it, that the most part of the fleet is grievously infected, and [men] die daily, falling sick in the ships by numbers; and that the ships of themselves be so infectious, and so corrupted, as it is thought to be a very plague; and we find that the fresh men that we draw into our ships are infected one day and die the next, so as many of the ships have hardly men enough to weigh their anchors; for my Lord Thomas Howard, my Lord

Sir John Hawkins, attributed to Hieronymus Custodis.

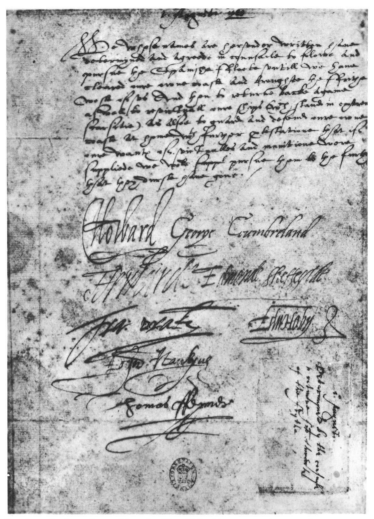

The Resolution signed by the English Commanders, 1 August 1588, after the defeat of the Armada off Gravelines. (*see page* 120)

A medal struck to commemorate victory over the Armada.

Sheffield, and some five or six other ships, being at Margate, and the wind ill for that road, are so weakly manned by the reason of this sickness, and mortality, as they were not able to weigh their anchors to come whereas we are.

Now, my Lords, sith the matter is of that moment for the service of her Majesty and this realm, we have entered into consideration what is fittest to be done, the extremity being so great; the one touching the service of the realm, the other concerning the mortality and sickness; and therefore thought this course which we here set down to be fittest to be done; which is: To divide our fleet into two parts; the one to ride in the Downs, as conveniently we can, the other ashore, and there to relieve them with fresh victuals, and to supply such other their wants as we can; and upon the hearing or discovery of the Spanish fleet, we shall be able, with the help of soldiers from the shore, for to be ready within a day for the service. And therefore, we are to pray your Lordships that Mr Quarles may be sent down with all speed unto us, with that money that should have prepared the next victualling.

My Lords, I must deliver unto your Lordships the great discontentments of men here, which I and the rest do perceive to be amongst them, who well hoped, after this so good service, to have received the whole pay, and finding it to come but this scantly unto them, it breeds a marvellous alteration amongst them; and therefore I do not see but, of present necessity, there must be order sent down for the payment of them unto 25 August; whereof I leave Sir John Hawkins to certify the Lord Treasurer in more particular from himself.

The *Roebuck* is not yet come to the fleet, but, as I understand, she is employed by my Lord of Huntingdon, whereby we are disappointed of the powder in her. And so I take my leave of your Lordships.

From Dover.

Howard

From Sir Francis Drake, to Sir Francis Walsingham, 23 August 1588

My judgment [is] that the Duke of Sidonia [with] his fleet shall jump with fair weather, the highest of a spring, [with] good wind, and the Duke of Parma embarking all in one day. If any one of these fail them, they shall never perform as much as they have promised to the King, their master. My reason is this. The most part of the ships of the Duke of Parma are small, and being pestered [crowded] with men of war, must of necessity have fair weather; and – as I am credibly given to understand – they must have a spring to bring their shipping both out of Dunkirk, Nieuport, and Sluys.

Now, for the Duke of Medina his fleet, there is [no] harbour for them upon that coast, so that to stir it requireth fair weather; which, when it happen that we should find them there, he is like, God willing, to have unquiet rest. And yet, with my consent, we ought much more to have regard unto the Duke of Parma and his soldiers than to the Duke of Sidonia, and his ships, for that our sands will take a strong party with us, against his great ships, under water. My poor opinion is that the Duke of Parma should be vigilantly looked upon for these twenty days, although the army of Spain return not this way; for of them I have no great doubt, although there be great cause for us all to watch carefully and defend mightily those many and proud enemies which seek to supplant the most honourable crown of England from our most gracious Sovereign, whom God defend, as he hath most graciously done for his great mercy's sake.

From aboard her Majesty's very good ship the *Revenge*.

Drake

I have sent to your Honour a copy, Englished, out of a letter sent from Don Pedro de Valdes to the [King his master] which doth deliver of some discontentment which was between the Duke and him.

Drake

From George Trenchard and Francis Hawley, Deputy-Vice Admirals in Dorset, to the Privy Council, 24 August 1588

Your Lordship's letter of the 27th of the last, touching the Spanish carrack, we . . . have performed your commandment in as much as in us lay, . . . thinking it also some part of our duties not to conceal from your Lordships the notable spoils that were made upon the ship, which came to Portland road seven days before our dealing therein; and much more had been if happily the Lord Admiral had not sent Mr Warner, a servant of his, before our coming, to take some care thereof; the disorder growing so far, as we could very hardly repress it ourselves, the great repair from all places being such.

... The carrack is so great as that she cannot be brought into this haven, and therefore we do attend your Lordships' direction what shall be done with her. She is much splitted, torn, and the charge will be great in keeping her here, for we are forced to keep therein ten persons continually to pump her for fear of sinking. Surely, in the stealing of her ropes and casks from her, and rotting and spoiling of sails and cables etc., the disorder was very great. It is credibly thought that there were in her 200 Venetian barrels of powder of some 120 [pounds] weight apiece, and yet but 141 were sent to the Lord Admiral. This very night some inkling came unto us that a chest of great weight should be found in the forepeak of the ship the Friday before our dealing. Of what credit it may be, as yet we know not; but do determine to examine the matter, and to send for the party that hath reported it. All search hath been made sithence our coming, but no treasure can be found, and yet we have removed some part of the ballast. We find here no Spaniards of any account, but only one who calleth himself Don Melchor de Pereda and nine others of the common sort; two Frenchmen, four Almains, and one Almain woman, and since their landing here, twelve more are dead. We humbly beseech your Lordships to give some speedy direction what shall be done with them, for that they are here diseased, naked, and chargeable.

The charges necessarily disbursed for the performing and discharging of this ship, her ordnance and loading, hath been so great, and so diversely disbursed, and yet unlevied, as we cannot presently particularise the same, but do think it will extend well near to £200, as by the accounts thereof, by the next messenger, shall to your Lordships particularly appear. And so we humbly take our leaves.

Weymouth,

George Trenchard
Fra. Hawley

In the coastal counties and shires the Lord High Admiral appointed vice-admirals, often from among his own relations. Their duties were many but lucrative. Survivors from captured or wrecked ships had to be examined, whatever their nationality, for foreign intelligence, which was at once sent to the Lord High Admiral or the Privy Council. In law the location of wrecks and prizes had to be reported to the vice-admiral or his deputies, who had to assess their value, send a tenth to the Lord High Admiral, and give judgement on the proper allocation of the rest, but often wrecks were pillaged and the proceeds spirited away before the authorities could do anything. The courts of Admiralty were besieged by suitors from all over Europe paying large fees to recover the value of goods seized on the high seas or in port. Many of the best families and richest merchants in England were engaged in 'privateering' and this anarchy in the Channel and western approaches the Spaniards had hoped to end.

From Sir John Gilbert and Sir George Carey, Member of Parliament for Hampshire, to the Privy Council, 26 August 1588

The said prisoners, being in number 397, whereof we sent to my Lord Lieutenant [the Earl of Bath] five of the chiefest of them, whom his Lordship hath committed to the town prison of Exon; and we have put 226 in our Bridewell, amongst which all the mariners are placed, which are 61, besides younkers and boys. The rest, which are 166, for the east of our country from the watching and guarding of them, and conveying of their provision of their victuals unto them – which was very burdensome unto our people in this time of harvest – we have therefore placed them aboard the Spanish ship, to live upon such victuals as do remain in the said ship; which is very little and bad, their fish unsavoury, and their bread full of worms, and of so small quantity as will suffice them but a very small time.

Greenwaye.

John Gilberte
Sir George Carey

From the Lord High Admiral, to Sir Francis Walsingham, 26 August 1588

I have received your letter of 24 August, touching the beer that was brewed at Sandwich. Mr Darrell hath been with me here, whom I have dealt withal; and I perceive it hath been refused, and upon that there were some appointed to taste it, and so found it to be sour, and yet he that hath the delivering of it – and so saith Mr Darrell too – that at the first it was good. But by like there was some great fault in the brewer, excuseth it by the want of hops. But, Sir, the mariners who

have a conceit (and I think it true, and so do all the captains here)
that sour drink hath been a great cause of this infection amongst us;
and, Sir, for my own part I know not which way to deal with the
mariners to make them rest contented with sour beer, for nothing
doth displease them more. There hath been heretofore brewed for the
navy here at Dover, as good beer as was brewed in London. This
service being in the Narrow Seas, and likely to continue, so long as
we have to do with the Low Countries, of necessity the victualling
must be here at Dover.

From aboard her Majesty's good ship the *Ark*.

Howard

From Sir John Hawkins, to William Cecil, Lord Burghley,
26 August 1588

The weather continueth so extreme and the tides come so swift
that we cannot get any victuals aboard but with trouble and difficulty, nor go from ship to ship. But as weather will serve, and time,
to gather better notes, your Lordship shall be more particularly
informed of all things.

From the *Ark Raleigh*, in Dover road.

Hawkins

There is a month's wages grown since 28 July, and ended 25
August, and so groweth daily till the discharge be concluded; therefore it were good your Lordship consider of it.

From the Lord High Admiral, to Sir Francis Walsingham,
27 August 1588

Upon your letter, I sent presently for Sir Francis Drake, and showed
him the desire that her Majesty had for the intercepting of the King's
treasure from the Indias [Indies]. And so we considered of it; and
neither of us finding any ships here in the fleet any ways able to go
such a voyage before they have been aground, which cannot be done
in any place but at Chatham; and now that this spring is so far past,
it will be fourteen days before they can be grounded. And where you
write that I should make nobody acquainted with it but Sir Francis
Drake – it is very strange to me that anybody can think that if it were
that [some] of the smallest barks were to be sent out, but that the

officers must know it; for this is not as if a man would send but over to the coast of France, I do assure you.

Sir Francis Drake, who is a man of judgment and best acquainted with it, will tell you what must be done for such a journey. Belike it is thought the islands be but hereby; it is not thought how the year is spent. I thought it good, therefore, to send with all speed Sir Francis, although he be not very well, to inform you rightly of all, and look what shall be there thought meet. I will do my endeavour with all the power I may; for I protest before God, I would give all that I have that it were met withal; for that blow after this he hath, would make him safe.

Sir, for Sir Thomas Morgan and the discharging of ships, I will deal withal when the spring is past; but before, I dare not venture. For them of London, I do not hear of them yet, but those that be with my cousin Knyvet.

Sir, I send you here enclosed a note of the money that Sir Francis Drake had aboard Don Pedro. I did take now, at my coming down, 3,000 pistolets, as I told you I would; for, by Jesus, I had not £3 besides in the world, and had not anything could get money in London; and I do assure you my plate was gone before. But I will repay it within ten days after my coming home. I pray you let her Majesty know so. And by the Lord God of Heaven, I had not one crown more; and had it not been mere necessity, I would not have touched one; but if I had not some to have bestowed upon some poor and miserable men, I should have wished myself out of the world. Sir, let me not live longer than I shall be most willing to all service, and to take any pains I can for her Majesty's service. I think Sir Francis Drake will say I have little rest day or night.

The *Ark*, in Dover road.

Howard

Enclosure:

   Treasure in the *Nuestra Señora del Rosario*

7,200
10,000
5,600
2,500
———
25,300

This I confess to have.

Carried aboard to my Lord Admiral, by his Lordship's commandment, the 23 August 1588, three thousand pistolets.

Drake
Howard

Taken out of the sum above written, by my Lord Admiral's
knowledge, three thousand pistolets, the 27 August, 1588.

Drake

From the Lord High Admiral, to William Cecil, Lord Burghley,
28 August 1588

My Lord, we have had here a wonderful storm these two days and it
continueth still. No man was able to come aboard of me for the
discharging of ships; so we were fain, with the wind and tide, and
not without peril, to come to Dover town, to confer about the
discharge of the ships and the appointing of those ships that shall
remain in the Narrow Seas under the charge of Sir Henry Palmer,
which is fit to be something strong for a time. My Lord, it is a
wonderful trouble the discharging. Things in this service hath grown
so intricate with charging and discharging.
    Dover.

Howard

From Sir John Hawkins, to William Cecil, Lord Burghley,
28 August 1588

I am sorry I do live so long to receive so sharp a letter from your
Lordship, considering how carefully I take care to do all for the best
and to ease charge. The ships that be in her Majesty's pay, such as I
have to do for, your Lordship hath many particulars of them and
their numbers; notwithstanding, I do send your Lordship all these
again. I had but one day to travail in, and then I discharged many
after the rate that I thought my money would reach; but after that
day I could hardly row from ship to ship, the weather hath been
continually so frightful.
    Here is victual sufficient, and I know not why any should be
provided after September, but for those which my Lord doth mean to
leave in the Narrow Seas; which numbers will be about a thousand
men, of which also I will send to your Lordship the names of the

ships and their particular numbers, and never omit it more, though I may ill do it always. I do not meddle with any of the ships of London, for my Lord will discharge them all; neither do I write your Lordship anything of the coast ships; but I am in gathering of a book of all those that served, and the quality and time of their service, as I can overcome it. Your Lordship shall see it in the best order I can. Some are discharged with fair words; some are so miserable and needy, that they are helpen with tickets to the victuallers for some victual to help them home; and some with a portion of money, such as my Lord Admiral will appoint, to relieve their sick men and to relieve some of the needy sort, to avoid exclamation. The sick men are paid and discharged, that are in her Majesty's pays; the soldiers also, for the most part, we discharge here; the retinues, some have leave to go to London, and are to be paid there; and thus there is left but convenient companies of mariners and gunners to bring home the ships to Chatham. Your Lordship may consider by the numbers and the time they are to pay to 25 August, I required 19,000 pound, which I perceive your Lordship hath paid. At that time I knew of no thorough discharge, and till then I never demanded any conduct in discharge. The time will come over somewhat also for a good company before they come to Chatham; but I will go with this as far as I can, and never demand more till extremity compel me.

I never yet knew any penny profit by sea books, nor know not what a dead pay meaneth, as it hath been most injuriously and falsely informed. There are diets to the captains, dead shares to the officers, and such like accustomed pays to the officers, which are paid, and no more. It shall hereafter be none offence to your Lordship that I do so much alone; for with God's favour I will and must leave all. I pray God I may end this account to her Majesty's and your Lordship's liking, and avoid my own undoing. If I had any enemy, I would wish him no more harm than the course of my troublesome and painful life; but hereunto, and to God's good providence, we are born.

I have showed your Lordship's letter to my Lord Admiral and Sir William Wynter, who can best judge of my care and painful travail, and the desire I have to ease the charge. Since we came to Harwich, the Margate, and Dover, our men have much fallen sick, whereby many are discharged; which we have not greatly desired to increase, because we always hoped of a general discharge; yet some mariners we have procured to divers of the ships, to refresh them. And so I leave in great haste, to trouble your Lordship.

From Dover.

Your honourable Lordship's humbly to command,

Hawkins

From Sir George Carey, to Sir Francis Walsingham, 29 August 1588

Having now brought the Spanish ship in safe harbour, bestowed the prisoners in sure keeping, and inventoried the ordnance and goods, we have sent unto your Honour the said inventory under our hands, with a note of the charges concerning the same, and with our humble request unto your Honours for some directions touching these Spanish prisoners, whom we would have been very glad they had been made water spaniels when they were first taken. Their provision, which is left to sustain them, is very little and nought, their fish savours, so that it is not to be eaten, and their bread full of worms. The people's charity unto them (coming with so wicked an intent) is very cold; so that if there be not order forthwith taken by your Lordships, they must starve. They are many in number, and divers of them already very weak, and some dead. The pilot of the ship is as perfect in our coasts as if he had been a native born. Divers of the rest are of the garrison [regiment] of Sicilia.

Cockington.

Sir George Carey

From Richard Tomson, Lieutenant of the *Margaret and John* of London, to the Privy Council, 8 September 1588

I certified Don Pedro de Valdes that the Lords of the Council were, of their honourable inclinations, intended to take some favourable courses for the releasing of the soldiers and mariners taken in his ship, by way of ransom, so far forth as he could procure some means for the levying of such sum of money as the same should arise unto, either by his letter to the Prince of Parma or any other his friends in the Low Countries, from whence the said ransom might be the most soonest provided.

Don Pedro, with the rest of the prisoners, seemed to be very glad that their Honours did vouchsafe them that favour, adding that it was a clemency sufficient to mollify the hardest heart of any enemy; that the news was as joyful unto them as if it had been tidings of their own liberty, in respect that the said poor people were raised by them and were their neighbours, and came in this employment for the love and zeal that they bare unto them; for that if they should perish by long imprisonment or other want, it would be unto them more grievous than all other accidents that might happen to themselves.

They all desire your Honours to continue this favourable mind to their poor men, of whose misery they stand in great doubt if they should remain in prison until the cold of the winter approacheth; and say that in having answer from your Honours what number shall be released, and for what sum, that then, your Honours giving leave, they will write to the Prince of Parma or the Spanish ambassador in France for the provision of the money.

At Esher, [Richard Drake's house] Sunday.

Richard Tomson

Examination of Prisoners, 9 September 1588

Interrogation of Spaniards taken in the Bay of Tralee:
There were twenty-four Spaniards taken in the Bay of Tralee, all of Castile and Biscay, which were executed because there was no safe keeping for them. They all agree that in the whole fleet there was only seven score and ten sail bound for Calais of purpose to have met with the Prince of Parma there, whereof when they failed, they determined to go for Flanders, but meeting her Majesty's fleet at sea, they were after a small fight, discomfited and dispersed.
Item, they say they lost in the fight only six sail and so afterwards [there] remaining but seventy sail, the rest being lost in the fight and dispersed, fell with the coast of Ireland, not knowing where they were, but resolved to return for Spain, but that they were kept back by contrary winds.
Item, they confess that there was aboard an Englishman called Don William, a man of a reasonable stature, bald, and very like Sir William Stanley. And that the said Don William is in one of the ships with the Duke of Medina Sidonia.

Item, they say that they lost the said Duke by tempestuous weather about eighteen days since, whom they think to be somewhere near to this coast.

Item, three of them offered ransoms for their lives promising that they would find friends in Waterford to redeem them, whose names they would not tell.

From Shannon.

From Sir John Popham, Attorney General, to William Cecil, Lord Burghley, 10 September 1588

For that it is taken to be important here to certify unto your Lordship and the rest of the Lords what hath happened here by the arrival of sundry of the ships of the Spanish fleet on the north west coast of this realm with all expedition, the Lord Chief Justice Anderson and others have thought it best to despatch away a servant of mine this bearer with the same in one of the barks stayed here for the Chief Justice's return into England. The advertisements are that on Thursday last and sithence that time there arrived first a bark which wrecked at the Bay of Tralee, another great ship being also now near that place. After that two great ships and one frigate at the Blasquets in the Sound there, seven other sail in the Shannon by Karryg-ni-Cowly, whereof two are taken to be of a thousand tons apiece, two more of 400 tons the piece, and three small barks. At the Lupus Head four great ships and towards the Bay of Galway four great ships more. It is thought that the rest of that fleet wherein the Duke of Medina Sidonia was, which were severed by a late tempest are also about some other part of this land. Before they were lost severed it seemeth by the Spaniards taken, there were not passing seventy sail left. The people in those parts are for the most part dangerously affected towards the Spaniards, but thanks be to God, that their power by her Majesty's good means, is shorter than it hath been, and that the Spaniards forces are so much weakened as they are, whereby there is no great doubt had here of any hurt that may grow thereby, although they use all the diligence and provision they may to provide for and prevent the worst of it.

From Cork,

Attorney General Sir John Popham

From Sir Richard Bingham, Governor of Connaught, to Lord
Deputy Fytzwylliam, 21 September 1588

I had intelligence sent me from my brother that the 700 Spaniards in
Ulster were despatched, which I know your Lordship heareth before
this time. And this I dare assure your Lordship now, that in a
fifteen or sixteen ships cast away on the coast of this province, which I
can in my own knowledge say to be so many, there hath perished at
least a 6,000 or 7,000 men, of which there hath been put to the
sword, first and last, by my brother George, and in Mayo, Thomond,
and Galway, and executed one way and another, about seven or
eight hundred, or upwards.

At Shrowle [Shrule, County Mayo],

Richard Bingham

From Sir Thomas Tresham, to the Privy Council, 22 October 1588

The humble protestation of my allegiance to her Majesty exhibited by
me unto Mr Dr Pearne, Dean of Ely, and Mr Dr Legge, Vice-
Chancellor of Cambridge, authorised by the lords of HM most
honourable Privy Council to receive the same. In the simplicity of
my heart, I do unfeignedly protest before the majesty of Almighty
God, that Queen Elizabeth is my undoubted sovereign lady and
queen *de iure et de facto*. I am religiously bounden in Christian duty to
endure her sacred highness' will and for no cause whatsoever to be
stirred to lift my hand against her Majesty, God's anointed. Finally,
if any shall attempt to murder, wound or hurt her Majesty, I, in true
subject-wise, will, to my uttermost might and ability, prosecute such
wicked wretch to death.

Ely,

Thomas Tresham

From Sir Thomas Tresham, to Lady Tresham, 2 November 1588

Jesu Maria. This present weeping All Souls' Day, which exceedeth
all the extreme wet days of this long matchless wettest season here
arrived my now kind, former unkind, cousin, accompanied with old
Brokesby and a pettifogging former solicitor of hers with a retinue of
many servants, I having none here but Hilton and my trusty cook.

From Hoxton.

Thomas

Minutes of the Privy Council, 3 November 1588. To the Arch-bishop of Canterbury

Letting his Lordship to understand that her Majesty's express pleasure and commandment was that order should be given by his Lordship in all the dioceses under his Lordship's province to the several days wherein all the realm might concur in giving public and general thanks unto God with all devotion and inward affection of hearts and humbleness for His gracious favour extended towards us in our deliverance and defence in the wonderful overthrow [and] destruction shewed by His mighty hand on our malicious enemies, the Spaniards, who had sought to invade and make a conquest of the realm.

The like letter written unto the Dean and Chapter of the Bishopric of York to take the same order within the diocese of that Bishopric as was in all points specified in the former letter.

From Sir George Carey, to the Privy Council, 5 November 1588

And during my abode there, having understanding that one of the Spanish fleet was cast on shore [at Hope near Salcombe], and the great pilfering and spoils that the country people made, I rode thither and took order for the restoring and rehaving again of all such things as either by search or inquiry I could find out, and have put the same in inventory. The ship is a hulk, and called *St Peter the Great*, one of those two ships which were appointed for the hospital to the whole navy. She is in burden, as they say, 550 tons, but I think not so much. The ship is not to be recovered; she lieth on a rock, and full of water to her upper decks. They confess that there were put into her, at her coming out of Spain, thirty mariners, a hundred soldiers, fifty appertaining to hospital. There are now remaining about a hundred forty, or thereabouts. There was put into her as much drugs and pothecary stuff as came to 6,000 ducats, of which I think there will come little good of the same, being in the water almost this sennight, the weather such as none could get aboard.

    Cockington.

Sir George Carey

From Sir Richard Bingham, to Elizabeth I, 3 December 1588

Their loss upon this province, first and last, and in several places, was twelve ships, which all we know of, and some two or three more supposed to be sunk to seaboard of the out isles; the men of which ships did all perish in the sea, save the number of 1,100 or upward, which we put to the sword; amongst whom there was divers gentlemen of quality and service, as captains, masters of ships, lieutenants, ensign-bearers, other inferior officers and young gentle-men, to the number of some fifty, whose names I have for the most part set down in a list, and have sent the same unto your Majesty; which being spared from the sword till order might be had from the Lord Deputy how to proceed against them, I had special direction sent me to see them executed as the rest were, only reserving alive one, Don Luis de Cordova [brother of the Marquis of Ayamonte], and a young gentleman, his nephew, till your Highness's pleasure be known.

From your Majesty's castle of Athlone.

Richard Bingham

CHAPTER EIGHT

Spoils of War: Retribution

Nuestras vidas son los ríos
que van a dar en la mar
que es el morir:
allí van los señorios
derechos a se acabar
y consumir.

Coplas por la muerte de su padre
JORGE MANRIQUE. (1440–1479)

(Our lives are the rivers that flow out into the sea, which is death.
These lordships go straight to their ends, to be consumed.)

*The Spanish officers, in spite of all the stress they had endured, preserved
during their retreat from Scotland a high degree of discipline. Food and drink
were running out and nowhere in northern latitudes could so large a number of
big ships put in for fresh supplies. Medina Sidonia had no alternative but to
order the captains to set course for Spain via the Orkneys and Ireland. Of
those who had sailed in July only about half got back to Spain. Of the senior
commanders who did so, all except Medina Sidonia and Martin de Bertendona
collapsed and died within a week of their arrival.*

*In Sligo Bay a Castilian soldier, Captain Cuellar, escaped from the
wreck of his ship and made his way into 'O'Rourke's Country'. O'Rourke,
being at war with the English, welcomed the help that Cuellar boldly gave
him. Few men in one summer's campaign can have faced death so often and
lived to tell the tale. This he does with dignity and humour, never having lost
faith either in God or himself.*

From the Marqués de Olivares, to Philip II, 27 June/8 July 1588

As it is now thirty-nine days since the Armada sailed, I am extremely
anxious that I have no news of it. If I recollect aright it was about this
date that your Majesty landed at Southampton [in 1554].

His Holiness is firm in his determination not to disburse a crown until the news arrives, and he is unyielding to the pressure I put upon him for money when he received the news that the Armada had sailed. As if your Majesty had not spent anything, or wanted the money for the purpose of hoarding it! The invariable reply of the Pope is, that as soon as the intelligence comes that the troops have landed, he will not fail to fulfil his part of the contract. He is gathering money from all quarters, so as not to be obliged to trench upon the sum in the Castle. He is furiously angry with your Majesty and with me. The way in which he now refuses the most just and usual things is exactly the same as his attitude a year ago when he thought that this bitter hour for him, having to part with his money, was approaching. I am doing my best to ensure the million (which surprises everyone) and so far as possible to prepare matters for the loan.

Rome,

Olivares

From the Duke of Medina Sidonia, to All Captains and Shipmasters, 25 July/4 August 1588

The course that is first to be held is to the NNE, until you be found under 61 degrees and a half; and then to take great heed lest you fall upon the island of Ireland, for fear of the harm that may happen unto you upon that coast. Then parting from those islands, and doubling the Cape in 61 degrees and a half, you shall run WSW until you be found under 58 degrees; and from thence to the SW to the height of 53 degrees; and then to the SSW, making to the Cape Finisterre, and so to procure your entrance into the Groyne or to Ferrol, or to any other port of the coast of Galicia.

Medina Sidonia

From Giovanni Mocenigo, Venetian Ambassador in Paris, (brother of Doge Alvise I Mocenigo), to the Doge & Senate, 30 July /9 August 1588

This morning the Spanish Agents publish the news, from Havre-de-Grace, that on Tuesday the Armada fell in with Drake near the Isle of Wight. Drake did all he could to take the land side, as also did the

Pope Sixtus V, 1521–1590, from a portrait in the Vatican.

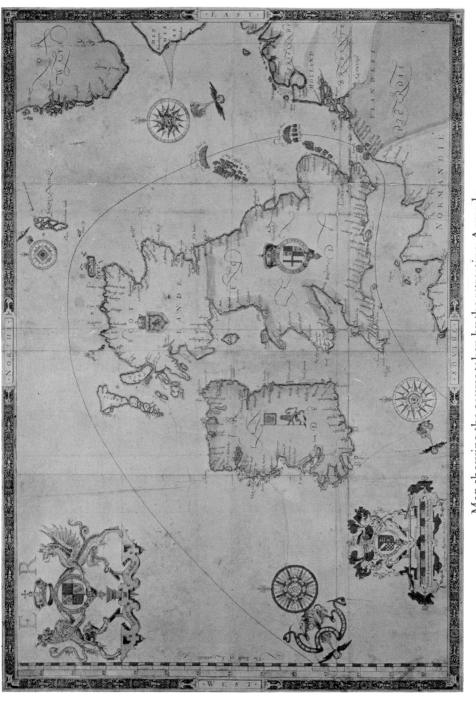

Map showing the course taken by the retreating Armada.

Spanish; they say the Spanish got the best of it after fighting a bit, sinking fifteen ships, among them the flagship; the rest fled towards Dover and Calais, where the body of the English fleet is lying. They add that three ships which had lost their masts were captured, and one large ship took fire. A Breton, who was taken by Drake and served on board one of his ships, has come home. He declares that a galleass attacked the flagship, and with the first broadside cut down her masts, and at the second sank her; and that Drake escaped in a boat under cover of the thick smoke. The English Ambassador has informed me that he disbelieves these Spanish reports for he has despatches from Rouen of the same date, announcing that the fleets were close together but had not attacked.

Paris,

Mocenigo

From Juan Manrique, to Juan d'Idiaquez, 1/11 August 1588

Many others will write to you the full details of the overthrow of the Armada, and I will therefore only say here that I pray to God to spare our good King to redress it, and you to aid him. Although you may think it bold on my part I cannot refrain from saying how the happiest expedition in the world has been defeated. The day on which we came to embark [in Flanders] we found the vessels still unfinished, not a pound of cannon on board, and nothing to eat. This was not because the Duke of Parma failed to use every possible effort, for it would be difficult to find another person in the world who works half as hard, but because both the seamen and those who had to carry out the details openly and undisguisedly directed their energies not to serve his Majesty, for that is not their aim, but to waste his substance and lengthen the duration of the war; besides which the common people threw obstacles in the way.

You must forgive me, but when I see the intentions of my sovereign thus badly fulfilled, I cannot help venturing to lay the matter before you. The general opinion here is that if his Majesty orders the remainder of the Armada to stay here, the enterprise would be much easier. God guide it all! We are all of us ready to die, and serve his Majesty as he may command. The Prince of Ascoli and Don Francisco de Toledo have arrived here, and the younger displays most distrust.

Don Jorge Manrique is here, and it is quite pitiable to see how he goes on.

For the love of God urge his Majesty to persevere in this enter⁄prise, for upon it depends mainly the ending of the war in Flanders; people here are delighted to see its postponement.

Dunkirk,

Juan Manrique

From Pedro de Valdes, General of the Andalusian Fleet, to Philip II, 21/31 August 1588

The 30th of last month I acquainted your Majesty with the proceed⁄ings of your fleet until that time; now I will write what hath since happened unto me. The same day the Duke called to council; and being within ten or twelve leagues of Plymouth, where, by the report of a fisherman whom we took we had understanding that the English fleet was at anchor, it was resolved we should make to the mouth of the haven and set upon the enemy, if it might be done with any advantage; or otherwise, keep our course directly to Dunkirk without losing of any time. Within two hours after, their fleet was discovered out of my ship four leagues off to leeward of ours, the haven of Plymouth remaining to windward of us. I acquainted the Duke withal presently, desiring to know what he thought fit to be done; wherein he neither took resolution nor made me answer, but, hoisting sail, spent all that day and night bearing but little sail, and by that means gave the enemy time to get the wind of us by next morning, who presently set upon our rearguard where Juan Martinez de Recalde and I did sail with the shipping under our charge. Our ordnance played a long while on both sides, without coming to hand stroke. There was little harm done, because the fight was far off.

When we had ended, I sent a pinnace unto Juan Martinez de Recalde, to know whether he had received any harm; his answer was that his galleon had been sore beaten, and that his foremast was hurt with a great shot; praying me that I would come to relieve him, for that other⁄ways he should not be able to abide any new fight if it were offered the same day. Whereupon making towards him with my ship, according to his desire, it happened that another Biscayan ship of his company, lying so in the way as I could neither pass by nor bear room, on the sudden fell foul in such sort with the prow of mine as she brake her spritsail and crossyard, by reason of which accident, and for want of sail, my ship being not able to steer readily, it happened again that, before I could repair that hurt, another ship fell foul with her likewise in the self same manner, and brake her bowsprit, halyards and forecourse. Whereupon, finding myself in so ill case I presently sent word thereof to the Duke, to the end he might stay for me until I had put on another forecourse, which I carried spare, and put myself in order.

In the meanwhile I got to the fleet as well as I could; and, being to leeward of them, struck the crossyard of my foremast and the rest of my sail, to repair my hurt the better, hoping that the Duke would have done according to my request. While I was in this case, the sea did rise in such sort that my ship, having struck sail and wanting her halyard of the foremast, being withal but badly built, did work so extremely as shortly after, and before it could be remedied, her foremast brake close by the hatches, and fell upon the mainmast, so as it was impossible to repair that hurt but in some good space of time. I did again send word thereof two several times to the Duke, and discharged three or four great pieces, to the end all the fleet might know what distress I was in, praying him either to appoint some ship or galleass to tow me ahead, or to direct me what other course I should take. Nevertheless, although he was near enough to me, and saw in what case I was, and might easily have relieved me, yet would he not do it; but even as if we had not been your Majesty's subjects nor employed in your service, discharged a piece to call the fleet together, and followed his course, leaving me comfortless in the sight of the whole fleet, the enemy being but a quarter of a league from me; who arrived upon the closing up of the day; and although some ships set upon me, I resisted them, and defended myself all that night, till the next day, hoping still that the Duke would send me some relief, and not use so great inhumanity and unthankfulness towards me; for greater I think was never heard of among men.

The next day, finding myself in so bad case, void of all hope to be relieved, out of sight of our fleet, and beset with the enemies, and Sir Francis Drake, admiral of the enemy's fleet, bearing towards me with his ship, from whom there came a message that I should yield myself upon assurance of good usage, I went aboard him, upon his word, to treat of the conditions of our yielding, wherein the best conclusion that could be taken was the safety of our lives and courteous entertainment;

for performance whereof he gave us his hand and word of a gentleman, and promised he would use us better than any others that
were come to his hands, and would be a mean that the Queen should
also do the like; whereupon, finding that this was our last and best
remedy, I thought good to accept of his offer. The next day he
brought me to see the general [Howard] by whom I was courteously
received, seeming to be sorry that the Duke had used me so hardly,
and confirming the same promises that Sir Francis Drake had made
unto me.

After ten days space that I had been in his company, he sent me to
London; and with me the captains of footmen, Don Alonso de
Cayas of Laja, and Don Vasco de Mendoca y de Silva of Xerez de
los Cavalleros, who had charge of the companies that were levied in
those places; and the Queen at his request sent us four leagues off to
a gentleman's house, called Richard Drake, that is his kinsman,
where we receive the best usage and entertainment that may be.
About forty of the better sort besides are bestowed in divers men's
houses in London; the rest together with the ship, were carried to
Plymouth.

I have no other matter to impart unto your Majesty until the return
of Sir Francis Drake, who is yet at sea, for then there will be some
resolution taken what shall become of us. These captains do humbly
kiss your Majesty's feet, and we all beseech your Majesty that it will
please you to remember us, and to comfort us with your princely
letters in answer hereof.

Valdes

From Giovanni Gritti, to the Doge & Senate, 24 August
/3 September 1588

I enclose a letter from the Duke of Parma.
  Rome,

Gritti

Enclosure: While standing on the look-out for the Armada of his
Majesty with all its ships, and considering how to carry out the
desired manoeuvre [of embarking], Captain Don Rodrigo de
Guzman arrived with letters from the Duke of Medina Sidonia,
announcing that he had sailed from Corunna on 22 July and was
now in twenty-four degrees of latitude (*sic*).

On 6 August Lieutenant Juan Gil arrived with despatches announcing that the Armada was abreast of Plymouth; that same evening Captain Pedro de León brought word that the fleet was off the Isle of Wight. They both stated that from the moment the Armada came abreast of Plymouth till the time they left the fleet, shots had been exchanged continually with the enemy who had been waiting them in Plymouth, and had let them pass ahead to join in a general action. The Duke of Medina Sidonia was unable to force on an action though he tried his best. One of his ships was burned and others which had carried away their masts, were lost though the crews were saved.

On the 7th came a pilot with news that the Armada was off Calais; whereupon the Duke of Parma left Bruges to hasten on the embarkation of his troops and to be nearer the Armada.

On the morning of the 8th came d'Areco, Secretary to the Duke of Medina Sidonia, with confirmation that the fleet was lying in the roads of S. Jean, close to Calais, and that although the enemy continued to harass them and fire shots, still the whole fleet was in excellent order and complete, though the Duke had not yet been able to force the enemy to come to an engagement as the wind was always against him.

The Duke of Parma left at once for Nieuport where the detachment of 12,000 men were to embark; and then came early to Dunkirk where everything was ready so that within that day the embarkation might have been carried out at Nieuport and at Dunkirk. At this juncture came the Superintendent-General Don Giorgio Manrique with further despatches of the day previous, explaining the danger to which the Armada was exposed if caught by a storm in the Channel, and urging the Duke of Parma to put out to sea with his ships and troops and to effect a junction with the Armada; so that in a body they might attack the enemy's fleet or secure a port for our own. This operation was impossible owing to the set of the wind which was such as to prevent even ships specially constructed for navigating those waters from putting out, to say nothing of the enemy's which barred the egress.

While the preparations for embarkation were rapidly progressing, the Prince of Ascoli and other personages arrived in Dunkirk on board a small ship; they had been commissioned by the Duke of Medina Sidonia to reunite all the ships which had been separated from the

Armada. They reported that on the morning of the 8th, very early, the enemy had sent eight fire-ships down upon our fleet, and although they had done no mischief, still the Duke of Medina Sidonia thought it well to give the order to cut the cables so as to avoid the danger. The fleet, finding itself thus free, and the same wind blowing as before, it was swept towards that part of the English coast which faces the north. The enemy did not miss the opportunity to give battle to some four ships which had become detached from the Armada. One of these, a galleass, went on shore under Calais, and a galleon on shore at Nieuport. For the rest our fleet will keep together and it is to be hoped that it will not receive any further damage, even if the wind prevented it from bearing down on the enemy. The Duke of Parma has all his men embarked and ready.

Dunkirk,

Parma

From Giovanni Gritti, to the Doge & Senate, 24 August /3 September 1588

His Holiness said to me that it was the work of God that the Turk should now be occupied in the Persian war. He talked of Hassan Pasha, and of the English Ambassador who had left Constantinople. 'The Queen of England' he remarked, 'has no need of the Turk to help her. Have you heard how Drake with his fleet has offered battle to the Armada? with what courage! do you think he showed any fear? He is a great captain'; and with that his Holiness went on to recount Drake's enterprises at San Domingo, at Cadiz, at Lisbon; the fleet he had captured; the riches he had acquired to his great glory. Then he proceeded to discuss the handling of the Armada; repeating his previous remarks, but adding two new points, all with his wonted remarkable frankness; first he said, 'that last year the Marquis of Santa Cruz refused to set sail from Spain, so as not to put himself under the Duke of Parma, and now, I hope to God that the Duke of Medina Sidonia has not been the cause of other difficulties by insisting that the Duke of Parma should come to meet him. For Sidonia was only a few hours distance from Parma, and the junction could easily have been effected, but it has not. The King of Spain exhausted himself by so much consideration for his captains; he is in straits for money which he is raising from Mantua, from the Archbishop of Toledo, a hundred thousand from Naples, the same from Sicily; we will send him five hundred thousand in fifteen days time, for five hundred thousand have been spent in fifteen days and yet were not sufficient.' And with that I took my leave.

Rome,

Gritti

From Marco Antonio Messia, Spanish agent in London, to the Magnificent Sir Alexander Ganavero [Philip II], 28 August /7 September 1588

It is publicly stated here that the Spanish prisoners confess they had orders, if they were victorious, to kill every Englishman over seven years old. They say they brought two kinds of whips, one for men and the other for women. In order that you may not think it strange for me to write you this, I send you two printed legends that are current here, one respecting the capture of Don Pedro de Valdes's ship, and the other about the Queen's visit to the army. I could send you a multitude of such things treating of the affairs of the fleet, and of men judged, and yet to be judged. When you have read them, and the relation about the Armada, please send them to Stafano Lercaro, with his packet. This is the reason these people are so enraged with the Spaniards. Their anger would certainly be justified if the above and other similar things were true.

London.

From Giovanni Mocenigo, to the Doge & Senate, 30 August/9 September 1588

The English fleet, on account of the great and continual storm, was unable to follow up the Spaniards, and has returned to England to provision itself, as it had begun to run somewhat short. Nothing is known about the Spanish Armada with certainty, although the Duke of Parma has sent out ships in various directions to gather news. The most experienced seamen think that it must be now off the coast of Norway, in great distress for provisions and munitions, and with its fittings riddled by artillery, or partly left in the sea when they cut their cables to fly from the fire ships. No one believes that the Armada will return to English waters; the English have been re-inforced both in men and ships, thanks to the advantage which they enjoy of being at home. This same view is taken by the Spanish themselves, who believe that the Armada, being unable to undertake any operations against England, will return to Spain, sailing round Ireland, in order to secure, as best they may, the remains of the fleet.

From Holland we learn that the Dutch were present at the capture of three Spanish galleons, and were so tempted by the booty which they made, that they have gone out with forty well-armed ships to hang upon the flank of the Spanish and to pick up any of the Armada which, by stress of weather or bad seamanship may become separated from the rest.

The Duke of Parma is dividing his army among the various fortresses, and all the nobility that was with him is being disbanded. He has had with him the most experienced captains and the finest troops drawn to his service by the desire for glory, and also because both rumour and the statements of the Spaniards represented the prizes as larger than have ever been heard of. The Spaniards, however, are not satisfied with the Duke; they accuse him of negligence and of little will to embark his troops so as to avoid placing himself under the command of the Duke of Medina Sidonia, and for fear of leaving the government of Flanders in the hands of Sidonia.

Paris,

Mocenigo

From Hieronimo Lippomano, to the Doge & Senate, 7/17 September 1588

The Ambassador [Mendoza, in Paris] affirms that the Queen and the whole country are in a panic, for only thirty ships have come home, and those very roughly handled; also that in various parts of the English army mutinies have broken out; and much more which, if true, your Serenity will already have heard from elsewhere.

We only know what is published here, and all letters and despatches pass into the hands of the King and Don Juan d'Idiaquez only. All I can say is that after the last news his Majesty was in excellent spirits, and so were his ministers.

These last news have caused the attacks on the Duke of Medina Sidonia to cease. They at first accused him of being the cause of all the disasters through his bad leadership, as, indeed they have openly accused the Duke of Parma of treachery to the King. His Majesty is very angry at these rumours, especially with Don Giorgio Manrique who has written a lot of lies, for the Duke of Parma has completely justified his conduct, and has demonstrated that he alone, with only small boats, was quite unable to cross over to England, as the Queen had other fifty ships lying in the river of London to repel a landing; nor was he able to effect a junction with the Armada after its arrival at Calais, for it was compelled to remove from its anchorage by the enemy's fire ships. The inventor of these ships was here in this Court for a long time, but no attention was paid to him, and in disgust he went into the service of the Queen of England.

Madrid,

Lippomano

From Giovanni Gritti, to the Doge & Senate, 14/24 September 1588

The Pope then took up the despatches which were lying on his table and read me the one from London by way of Lyons saying the Armada, reduced to ninety sail, is in Scotch waters. It endeavoured to secure a port from the King of Scotland, but failed. His Holiness said that from Turin, on the other hand, he had news that the Armada had secured a port, had defeated Drake and driven him to seek refuge in the Thames. 'One day', he added, 'we shall know the truth.' The positive information which his Holiness gave me was that there was jealousy between Medina Sidonia and Parma because Medina Sidonia would not obey Parma in land operations as the King wished and had ordered; and, further that Sidonia insisted that Parma should come to join him, and follow him in his attack on Drake, although Parma had ships which were fit for nothing but for transporting his troops from one shore to the other. This quarrel between the leaders was no new thing of the moment, but began in the days of the Marquis of Santa Cruz, who for this reason would never sail on the English enterprise.

Rome,

Gritti

From Hieronimo Lippomano, to the Doge & Senate, 19/29 September 1588

On the 23rd of this month Don Balthasar de Zuñica arrived at the

Escorial; he had been despatched by the Duke of Medina Sidonia on 20 August, while the Armada was off the Orkneys, in sixty degrees of latitude. He made a report of all that had taken place since the fleet left Calais, and of the bad state in which it was at present. [Copy enclosed]

His Majesty feels these misfortunes profoundly, but shows that he is more than ever determined to follow out his enterprise with all the forces at his disposal. He is resolved that by March next a most powerful fleet shall be ready to put to sea. Orders will be sent out to raise men in Italy and also in Spain. All ships of every build will be seized, all the corn throughout Spain will be made into biscuits, and every other sort of provision will be got ready. Six ships with provisions have sailed from Lisbon for Corunna, and another six in their company, and this will be a most useful reinforcement when the Armada comes into that port. His Majesty has given orders to build in Lisbon twenty galleys fit to sail in English waters; they are to be shorter and higher than the usual model, and already the wood is prepared.

Madrid,

Lippomano

Enclosure:

Our fleet left Calais through fear of the enemy's fire ships and made for the open sea in the endeavour to avoid the mouth of the channel. God wished to punish us for our sins, and more to that than to aught else must be attributed the fact that the wind was in our teeth, and kept blowing up so strongly that, all against our will, we were forced into the channel with the enemy always to windward of us.

On Monday morning the enemy, having reconnoitred our fleet, drew out with his own and began to chase thirty of our ships along the coast by Calais, keeping along the shore and trying to drive them away from it. The rest of their fleet, in order of battle, bore down on us, and began a furious infernal cannonade. The battle lasted about nine hours, in my judgment. This ship and the *San Matheo* have been so badly damaged that of the few survivors some were transhipped with the Adjutante Don Francesco di Toledo and Don Diego Pimentel. The *San Matheo* is held for lost.

Another ship, a Biscayan, called the *María Juan*, went to the bottom. Her captain, Castion, was saved along with a Navarese gentleman, called Don Gasparo d'Espoletta, all burned about the face, as a page of his told me. Don Martín and Don Juan di Viamonte, sons of the Medinetta, perished with her.

The enemy's fleet numbered upwards of one hundred and thirty sail. The flag-ship of the galleasses, which made for Calais, was attacked and cannonaded; we do not know if she was captured; for my part I think so, and we saw that the castle of Calais fired its guns and tried to shelter the galleass.

Don Felippe di Cordova perished; may God pardon him; so too Don Pedro di Mendoza and other gentlemen, soldiers, gunners, mariners in great numbers, all from the district of Carrion; others went to the bottom. It was a distressing spectacle which we have seen these last few days.

There are many who think that in two days more than 1,700 shots were fired. No one of importance was killed.

On Wednesday, 8 August, in the morning the enemy came out against us so vigorously and so arrogantly, that our leader had some apprehensions, but the grace of God miraculously favoured us. On this day the enemy won the advantage owing to the disorder in which we sailed, the bad weather, and the fear of the last action, in which the Duke, with four other ships, while leading the fleet was so hard pressed that we thought our destruction had come. Fortune was not content with giving us a single foe, she brought out the Flanders galleys as well. The enemy then turned off, took the windward of us, and continued his course in perfect order, and never letting our rear-guard out of sight but keeping just out of cannon shot; and thus he followed us for all Wednesday, Thursday and Friday.

On that day, at nightfall, the enemy forced us back, and on Saturday morning he drew up in order of battle, and came down upon us, but keeping just out of range; and as we stood waiting the onset the enemy made a tack, stood out to open sea, and gradually drew away from us so that by sundown he was out of sight.

Our route outside Scotland is long; pray God we come safe home. It is the historian's business to comment on events. I reserve all remarks till I arrive at Court, when there will be much to say. For myself I can only add that I am very hungry and thirsty, for no one has more than a half pint of wine and a whole one of water each day; and the water you cannot drink for it smells worse than musk. It is more than ten days since I drank any. The voyage is not so short but that there remain to us four hundred leagues of road. They say we are to go straight to Corunna, and the troops are to be lodged in Galicia.

The Gulf of Scalloway, 20 August 1588; in 60 degrees of high latitude.

From Hieronimo Lippomano, to the Doge & Senate, 29 September/ 1 October 1588

The Armada begins to reach the coast of Spain; it is in a very bad plight, to say the truth, the result of the enemy's attacks and the long voyage. They calculate that from the time when they left Lisbon they have sailed five thousand miles. The three Venetians are all safe. I have no other news except that the Commander-in-Chief complains loudly of some captains, and has hung one and is trying others for refusing to fight and deserting.

The King has today proposed to the Cortes to levy a tax of one real per sack of corn ground. Though Spain is in great straits, the King will not be able to abandon the enterprise against England. A loan of a million of gold has been raised today, and the Viceroy of Italy and the Governor of Milan are instructed to ask for a large donation. But as no one is paid, as the King gives no audience and does not despatch business, the cry of his people goes up to heaven; and Father Marian Azzaro, who speaks very frankly, said to the King the other day, that, although his prayers and processions were very good things, yet it was certain that God gave ear to other voices before his; when the King asked 'what voices', Father Marian replied, 'those of the poor oppressed who stay about the Court in pain, without being paid and without having their business attended to'.

At this moment a courier has arrived with news that the Duke of Medina Sidonia, who is in ill-health, reached Santander in Biscay, on the 20th of last month; he has twenty-four ships all in a bad way; and especially on board of one all have died of famine and misery. Don Alonso de Leyva has been left behind in a storm. The King has ordered all the ships to Corunna, for repairs. They say that there are serious differences between the Duke of Medina Sidonia and the Duke of Parma each one trying to throw the blame on the other.

Madrid,

Lippomano

From Marco Antonio Messia in London, Agent's Report, 29 September/1 October 1588

They say that there are several ships of the Armada in Ireland, but they tell the story so variously that I know not what to believe. Some say that, after the ships had reached Spain, contrary winds forced them back to Ireland, where they were wrecked. Some men from them were said to have been saved and they were captured and hanged by a Captain Denny [Sir Edward Denny], on account of some special hatred he bore against Spaniards, in consequence of his once having had a colonel for a prisoner of his in Ireland [Col. Sebastiano di San Joseph], who was assisted to escape by Don Bernardino de Mendoza, then Spanish ambassador in England. Others say that the Spaniards have joined the savages of the island, and have fortified themselves inland.

On Thursday last a Spaniard died in Bridewell, called something de la Cerda [Don Alonso de la Serna], who, they say, was a brother-in-law of the Englishman Don William [William Stanley], who was saved from the ship in consequence of his having been sent, shortly before she was taken, on an errand from Don Pedro de Valdes to the duke. I expect more of them will die unless something be done for them, as there are many sick and they get no care. The Italians have given them alms freely, but there are so many of them that a very small sum falls to each one. From my heart I recommend their case.

From Hieronimo Lippomano, to the Doge & Senate, 25 September/ 5 October 1588

I wrote to your Serenity announcing the arrival first of Captain Oquendo with ten ships at San Sebastian, then of the Duke of Medina Sidonia with twenty-four at Santander in Galicia. I am now informed that ten more ships have reached the coast; nothing has been heard as yet of Don Alonso de Leyva, of Don Martín de Recalde, and other commanders, with upwards of fifty vessels which became separated from the rest by a great storm. They think that they may have gone to the Azores, which would be the least disastrous thing that could happen, for it is known that they were very much damaged and without food.

Comments are very various, and the whole expedition is considered very difficult. For, supposing that they refit the Armada and send it off again to join the forces in Flanders, then it will run precisely the same dangers as it has met this year. If they determine to make the muster of the whole armament in Spain, then there is the difficulty of transporting the Flanders veterans to Spain. Then but small account can be made of the survivors of the Armada, for almost all on their return fall ill, many die and many, in spite of precautions, succeed in deserting, and only today news has arrived that Captain Oquendo, a brave soldier and brother of the Marqués de Vigliena, along with other commanders and persons of quality, died at once on reaching land.

Madrid,

Lippomano

From Hieronimo Lippomano, to the Doge & Senate, 5/15 October 1588

Don Juan d'Idiaquez and Don Christoforo de Mora are in perpetual consultation as to the best means for carrying out effectively an expedition against England in the coming year. But now more than ever all those obstacles which I have so frequently indicated, are made apparent, especially since the return of the Duke of Medina Sidonia to Spain. I am assured, however, that they have resolved to put together a powerful armament without any regard to the cost; to change the Commander-in-Chief; to alter the whole plan of campaign, as they now recognise many errors and many fallacious presuppositions in the plan of this year's campaign. They hold that the most important point of all is the possession of harbours in which at least a part of the Armada can take shelter. The King of France has shown a friendly disposition by offering to give the Armada every help he could at Calais and elsewhere, and they accordingly propose to ask his most Christian Majesty, in confirmation of his kind disposition, to grant the use of French ports to the Spanish Armada; they promise that if he does so he will not only be acting in a way which is worthy of his title of most Christian, but that he will enjoy the merit of having assisted in an enterprise which must approve itself to God; and the King of Spain will acknowledge his help and endeavour to repay it on all occasions. His Majesty has also been advised that if the Queen of England would abandon the protectorate of Zealand and Holland by restoring the fortresses, it would be as well to conclude a treaty with her and so put an end to all these expenses and troubles. And it would be no dishonour to the King, who in this way would have achieved the principal object for which he undertook this war, namely, the recovery of those provinces. Those who urge this line of action say that the Queen of England will in all probability be ready to agree to these terms, for she feels that she has acquired great glory by having, this year, defended her kingdom so successfully against all the power of Spain; and she will not care to risk this reputation and continue in so dangerous a position; for she must expect a most formidable attack next year, while she lacks the men, money, and means to resist it. I hear, however, that his Majesty is not favourable to this idea.

Don Bernardino de Mendoza, hearing that the King is little satisfied with his conduct and especially for the false reports which he scattered about, has asked leave to retire; he alleges that he is nearly blind and therefore no longer fit for service. It is thought that in a few days his request will be granted, chiefly with a view to satisfying his most Christian Majesty who looks on Don Bernardino's reckless character with little favour.

Madrid,

Lippomano

From Hieronimo Lippomano, to the Doge & Senate, 4/14 February 1589

Don Pedro de Valdes, prisoner in England, who was captured at the mouth of the Channel, because his ship carried away her mast and fell behind, has now implored the King for the love of justice to condemn the Duke of Medina Sidonia to pay his ransom and, the ransom of all the ship's company, because the Duke refused to come to his rescue as he might quite easily have done. The King has endorsed the petition with his own hand and said that the case shall proceed. And so they are now beginning an action against the Duke, not merely for this, but for many other mistakes.

Madrid,

Lippomano

Envoi

El austro proceloso airado suena,
crece su furia, y la tormenta crece,
y en los hombros de Atlante se estremece
el alto Olimpo y con espanto truena;
mas luego vi romperse el negro velo
deshecho en agua, y a su luz primera
restituirse alegre el claro dia,
y de nuevo esplandor ornado el cielo.
Miré, y dije: 'Quien sabe si le espera
igual mudanza á la fortuna mía?'
           La tempestad y la calma
                      JUAN DE ARGUIJO. (1565–1623)

(The perilous south wind roars angrily, its fury rises, and with it a tempest; tall Olympus shakes on the shoulders of Atlas, and thunders in alarm. But later I saw the black veil break, dissolving into water, and the clear day happily restored to its original brightness, and gazing on the sky lovely with a new splendour, I said: 'Who knows if a like sign of hope will not mark a change in my fortunes?')

From Captain Francisco de Cuellar, to a friend in Spain [unnamed], 24 September/4 October 1589

I believe that you will be astonished at seeing this letter on account of the slight certainty that could have existed as to my being alive. That you may be quite sure of this I write it and at some length, for which there is sufficient reason in the great hardships and misfortunes I have passed through since the Armada sailed from Lisbon for England, from which the Lord in His infinite good pleasure delivered me. I have not had the opportunity to write to you for more than a year and I have not done so until now that God has brought me to these States of Flanders where I arrived twelve days ago with the Spaniards who escaped from the ships that were lost in Ireland, Scotland and Shetland, which were more than twenty of the largest in the Armada.

A gold cross recently recovered from the wreck of the Girona.
It belonged to one of the Knights of the Order of St. John, Malta,
probably her captain, Fabricio Spinola.

A sea astrolabe, found in 1845 on the shore at Valencia, Eire, and believed to have belonged to one of the three Spanish ships wrecked there in 1588.

Three Spanish men-of-war in a storm; an engraving by Huys after Pieter Breughel I, c. 1565.

The galleon *San Pedro*, in which I sailed, received much injury from many heavy cannon balls which the enemy lodged in her in various parts, and although they were repaired as well as was possible at the time, there were still some hidden shot-holes through which much water entered. After the fierce engagement we had off Calais on 8 August, continuing from the morning till seven o'clock in the evening – which was the last of all – our Armada being in the act of retiring – oh! I don't know how I can say it – the fleet of our enemy followed behind to drive us from their country; and when it was accomplished and everything safe, which was the 10th of the same month, seeing that the enemy had stopped [ceased to follow], some of the ships of our Armada trimmed up and repaired their damage.

On this day, for my great sins, I was resting for a little as for ten days I had not slept nor ceased to assist at whatever was necessary for me, a pilot, a bad man whom I had, without saying anything to me, made sail and passed out in advance of the Admiral's ship for about two miles, as other ships had done, in order to effect repairs. When about to lower sail to see where the galleon was leaking a tender came alongside and summoned me on the part of the Duke [of Medina Sidonia] to go on board the Admiral's ship. I proceeded thither, but before I reached her, orders were given in another ship that I and another gentleman, Don Cristóbal de Avila, who went as captain of a store ship – which was far ahead of the galleon – should be put to death in the most ignominious fashion.

When I heard of this severity, I thought I should have burst with passion, saying that all should bear me witness of the great wrong done to me, I having served so well, as could be seen by written document. The Duke heard nothing of all this, because, as I say, he had retired and would see no one. Señor Don Francisco Bovadilla alone was he who ordered and countermanded in the Armada; and by him, and others, whose evil deeds are well known, all was managed. He ordered me to be taken to the ship of the Auditor [Judge Advocate General] that his advice should be carried out on me. I went there; and, although he was severe, the Auditor, Martin de Aranda, heard me and obtained confidential information concerning me. He discovered that I had served his Majesty as a good soldier, for which reason he did not venture to carry out on me the order that had been given him. He wrote to the Duke about it, that if he did not order him in writing and signed with his own hand, he would not execute that order, because he saw that I was not at fault, nor was there cause for it. Accompanying it I wrote a letter to the Duke of such a nature that it made him consider the affair carefully, and he replied to the Auditor that he should not execute the order upon me, but on Don Cristóbal, whom they hanged with great cruelty and ignominy, being a gentleman and well known. The Auditor was very courteous to me [throughout the affair] because of the great respect he had for those who were in the right. I remained in his ship in which we were in imminent danger of death because she opened so much with a storm which sprang up that she continually filled with water, and we could not dry her out with the pumps. We had neither remedy nor succour, except it was from God; for the Duke did not appear, and all the Armada proceeded, scattered in such manner by the storm that some ships went to Germany, others drove on the islands of Holland and Zealand into enemy hands, others went to Shetland, others to Scotland, where they were lost and burned. More than twenty were lost in the kingdom of Ireland, with all the chivalry and flower of the Armada. The ship I sailed in was from the Levant, to which were attached two others, very large, to afford us aid if they could. In these came Don Diego Enriquez, 'the hunchback', as Maestre de Campo, and not being able to weather Cape Clear [actually Erris Head on the Mayo coast] in Ireland, on account of the severe storm which arose upon the bow, he was forced to make for the land with these three ships which, as I say, were of the largest size, and to anchor more than half a league from the shore [in Sligo Bay], where we remained for four days without being able to make any provision. On the fifth day there sprang up so great a storm on our beam with a sea up to the heavens, so that the cables could not hold nor the sails serve us, and we were driven ashore with all three ships upon a beach, covered with very fine sand, shut in on one side and the other by great rocks [Streedagh Strand]. Such a thing was never seen: for within the space of an hour all three ships were broken in pieces so that there did not escape 300 men, and more than 1,000 were drowned, among them many persons of importance – captains, gentlemen, and other officials.

Don Diego Enriquez died there one of the saddest deaths that has ever been seen in the world. In consequence of fearing the very heavy sea that was washing over the highest part of the wrecks, he took his

ship's boat that was decked, and he and the son of the Count of Villa
Franca and two other Portuguese gentlemen, with more than 16,000
ducats, in jewels and crown-pieces, placed themselves under the deck
of the said boat, and gave the order to close and caulk the hatchway
by which they had entered. Thereupon more than seventy men, who
had remained alive, jumped from the ship into the boat, and while
she was making for the land so great a wave washed over her that she
sank and all on board were swept away. Then she drifted along,
rolling over in different directions with the waves until she went
ashore, where she settled wrong side up, and by these mischances the
gentlemen who had placed themselves under the deck died within.
More than a day and a half after she had grounded, some savages
arrived, who turned her up for the purpose of extracting nails or
pieces of iron; and breaking through the deck, they drew out the
dead men. Don Diego Enriquez expired in their hands, and they
stripped him and took away the jewels and money which they (the
dead men) had, casting the bodies aside without burying them.

I placed myself on the top of the poop of my ship, after having
commended myself to God and Our Lady, and from thence I gazed
at the terrible spectacle. Many were drowning in the ships, others,
casting themselves into the water, sank to the bottom without returning to the surface; others on rafts and barrels, and gentlemen on
pieces of timber; others cried out aloud in the ships calling upon
God; captains threw their jewelled chains and crown-pieces into the
sea; the waves swept others away, washing them out of the ships.
While I was watching this sorrowful scene, I did not know what to
do, nor what means to adopt as I did not know how to swim and the
waves and storm were very great; and, on the other hand, the land
and the shore were full of enemies, who went about jumping and
dancing with delight at our misfortunes; and when any one of our
people reached the beach two hundred savages and other enemies
fell upon him and stripped him of what he had on until he was left
in his naked skin. Such they maltreated and wounded without pity,
all of which was plainly visible from the battered ships.

I went to the Auditor – God pardon him! – he was very sorrowful
and depressed, and I said to him that he should make some provision
for saving his life before the ship went to pieces, as she could not last
for half a quarter of an hour longer; nor did she last it. Most of her
complement of men and all the captains and officers were already

drowned and dead when I determined to seek means of safety for my life, and placed myself upon a piece of the ship that had broken off, and the Auditor followed me, loaded with crown-pieces which he carried stitched up in his waistcoat and trousers. There was no way to detach the portion of wreck from the ship's side, as it was held fast by some heavy iron chains and the sea and the pieces of timber floating about loose struck it, nearly killing us. I managed to find another resource which was to take the cover of a hatchway, about as large as a good-sized table that by chance the mercy of God brought to my hand. When I tried to place myself upon it, it sank with me to a depth of six times my height below the surface, and I swallowed so much water that I was nearly drowned. When I came up again, I called to the Auditor, and I managed to get him upon the hatchway cover with myself. In the act of casting off from the ship there came a huge wave breaking over us in such a manner that the Auditor was unable to resist it, and the wave bore him away and drowned him, crying out and calling upon God while drowning. I could not aid him as the hatchway cover, being without weight at one end began to turn over with me and at that moment a piece of timber crushed my legs. With great exertion, I righted myself upon my supporting timber; and, supplicating Our Lady of Ontanar, there came four waves, one after the other, and without knowing how, or knowing how to swim, they cast me upon the shore, where I emerged, unable to stand, all covered with blood and very much injured.

The enemies and savages, who were on the beach stripping those who had been able to reach it by swimming, did not touch me, seeing me, as I have said, with my legs and hands and my linen trousers covered with blood. In this condition I proceeded little by little, as I could, meeting many Spaniards stripped to the skin, without any kind of clothing whatsoever on them, chattering with the cold, which was severe, and thus I stopped for the night in a deserted place, and was forced to lie down upon some rushes on the ground, with the great pain I suffered in my leg. Presently a gentle-man came up to me, a very nice young fellow, quite naked, and he was so dazed that he could not speak, not even to tell me who he was; and at that time which would be about nine o'clock at night, the wind was calm and the sea subsiding. I was then wet through to the skin, dying with pain and hunger, when there came up two people – one of them armed and the other with a large iron axe in his hands – and upon reaching me and the other man who was with me, we remained silent, as if we had not anything amiss with us. They were sorry to see us; and without speaking a word to us, cut a quantity of rushes and grass, covered us well, and then betook them-selves to the shore to plunder and break open money-chests and whatever they might find, at which work more than 2,000 savages and Englishmen who were stationed in garrisons near there, took part.

Managing to rest a little, I began to doze; and when fast asleep, at about one o'clock in the night, I was disturbed by a great noise of men on horseback – there were more than two hundred of them – who were going to plunder and destroy the ships. I turned to call my companion, to see if he slept, and found he was dead, which occasioned me great affliction and grief. I got to know afterwards he was a man of position. There he lay on the ground with more than six hundred other dead bodies which the sea cast up, and the crows and wolves devoured them, without their being anyone to bury them.

At dawn I began to walk, little by little, searching for a monastery of monks, that I might repair to it as best I could, and I arrived with much trouble and toil. I found it deserted and the church and images of the saints burned and completely ruined, and twelve Spaniards hanging within the church by the act of the Lutheran English, who went about searching for us to make an end of all of us who had escaped. All the monks had fled to the woods for fear of the enemy, who would have sacrificed them as well if they had caught them, as they were accustomed to do, leaving neither place of worship nor hermitage standing; for they demolished them all, and made them drinking places for cows and swine.

[Later] that day I met a woman of more than eighty years of age who was driving off five or six cows to hide them in a wood, so that the English who had come to stay in her village might not take them. As she saw me she stopped and said 'Thou Spain?' I said 'Yes' by signs and that I had been shipwrecked. She began to lament much and to weep, making me signs that I was near her house but not to go there as there were numerous enemies in it, and they had cut off the heads of many Spaniards. At last with the information of the old woman, I decided to go to the shore where the ships lay that had been wrecked three days before, where many parties of people went about

casting away and removing to their huts all our effects. I saw two
poor Spanish soldiers approaching stripped naked as when they were
born, crying out and calling upon God to help them. They came to
me, as I called to them from the place where I was concealed, and
recounted to me the cruel deaths and punishments which the
English had inflicted upon more than a hundred Spaniards they had
taken. I said, 'Let us proceed to the ships where these people are
going about plundering, perhaps we shall find something to eat and
drink for it is certain that I shall die of hunger.' And going in that
direction we began to see dead bodies which the sea continued to
cast up. There were stretched out upon that strand more than four
hundred, among whom we recognised some, including poor Don
Diego Enriquez, whom, with all my sad plight, I did not wish to
pass by without burying him in a pit, which we made in the sand at
the water's edge. We laid him there, along with another very
honourable captain, a great friend of mine, and we had not quite
finished burying them, when there came up to us two hundred
savages to see what we were doing. We said to them by signs that we
were placing there those men who were our brothers, that the crows
might not eat them. Then we went off and searched for something to
eat along the shore – of biscuits which the sea was casting up, when
four savages came up. [Their chief] by the grace of God assisted me
and my two companions and brought us away from there and put
us on a road which led from the coast to a village where they lived.
My poor companions were naked and freezing with the cold, which
was very great; and not being able to exist nor to assist me, they went
in front by the road and I reached a height from which I caught sight
of some huts of straw and going towards them by a valley, I entered
a wood [where] an old savage of more than seventy years came out
from behind the rocks, and two young men with their arms – one
English, the other French – and a girl of the age of twenty years most
beautiful, who were all going to the shore to plunder. The Englishman came up, saying 'Yield Spanish poltroon' and made a slash at
me with a knife, desiring to kill me. I warded off the blow with a
stick I carried in my hand, but in the end he got me and cut the
sinew of my right leg. He went to repeat the blow immediately, had
not the savage come up with his daughter, who may have been the
Englishman's mistress. They took him away from me, and the savage
began to strip me, to the taking off of my shirt under which I wore a

gold chain of the value of more than 1,000 reals. When they saw it, they rejoiced greatly and searched the jacket, thread by thread, in which I carried forty-five gold crowns, and when the Englishman saw that I carried a chain and gold crowns, he wanted to take me prisoner, saying that he would probably be offered a ransom for me. I replied that I was a very poor soldier and had gained what they saw in the ship. The girl lamented much to see the bad treatment I received and asked them to leave me the clothes and not to injure me any more. I remained among the trees, bleeding from the wound the Englishman had inflicted. I proceeded to put my jacket and sacking shirt on again. They had taken away my shirt and some relics of great value belonging to the Order of the Holy Trinity which I wore inside a small vest. They had been given me at Lisbon, and these the savage damsel took and hung them round her neck, making me a sign that she wished to keep them, saying to me that she was a Christian: which she was in like manner as Mahomet. From the hut they sent me a boy with a poultice made of herbs to put on my wound, and butter and milk and a small piece of oaten bread to eat. When the boy was about to turn back, he told me to continue travelling straight towards some mountains that appeared to be about six leagues off behind which there were good lands belonging to an important savage very friendly to the King of Spain; and that he gave shelter to, and treated well, all the Spaniards who went to him; and that he had in his village more than eighty of those from the ships. At this news I took some courage. That night I reached some huts where they did not do me harm because there was in them one who knew Latin [who] dressed my wound, gave me supper and a place where I might sleep upon some straw. In the middle of the night his father and brothers arrived, loaded with plunder and our things, and it did not displease the old man that I had been sheltered in his house and well treated. In the morning they gave me a horse and a boy to convey me over a mile of bad road with mud up to the girths. We heard a very great noise and the boy said to me by signs, 'Save yourself, Spain, many Sassana horsemen are coming this way.' He took me away to hide among the rocks where we were very well concealed. There were about a hundred and fifty horsemen going back to the coast to plunder as many Spaniards as they found. God delivered me from them, and proceeding on our way, there fell in with me more than forty savages on foot, and they wished to make

little pieces of me because they were all Lutherans. They did not do
it, as the boy, who came with me told them that his master had taken
me prisoner and that he had me in custody and had sent me on the
horse to be cured. Reaching the mountain range that they gave me for
direction, I met with a lake round which there were about thirty
huts, all forsaken and unoccupied. Not knowing where to go, I
sought out the best hut. On entering the door, I saw it full of sheaves
of oats, which is the ordinary bread these savages eat, and I gave
thanks to God, but just then I saw three men emerge from one side,
naked as when their mothers brought them forth and they stood up
and stared at me. They gave me a fright, for I thought they were,
without doubt, devils, and they understood no less that I might be so,
swathed in my ferns and matting. As I entered they did not speak to
me, because they were quaking, nor, any more, did I to them. The
hut being somewhat dark I said: 'Oh Mother of God, be with me
and deliver me from all evil.' When they heard me speaking Spanish,
they also said 'Let that great Lady be with us.' I felt reassured and
went up to them asking them if they were Spaniards. 'Yes, we are,
for our sins,' they replied, 'Eleven of us were stripped together on the
shore and we came to seek some land of Christians. On the way we
met an enemy party who killed eight of us, and the three who are here
made our escape through a wood so thick that they could not discover
us.' I said to them, 'Be of good courage, commend yourselves to the
Lord, near to where we are there is a land of friends and Christians,
a village three or four leagues distant that belongs to Señor de
Ruerque [O'Rourke] where they have sheltered many of our lost
Spaniards.' The poor fellows rejoiced and asked me who I was. I
told them I was Captain Cuellar. They could not believe it because
they had felt sure I was drowned; and they came up to me and
almost completely killed me with embraces. One of them was an
ensign and the other two private soldiers. We slept without supping,
not having eaten anything but blackberries and water-cresses.

[After a day in hiding] we sent along in the mud, and dying with
hunger, thirst and pain, until God was pleased to bring us to a land
of some safety where we found huts of better people, who although
all savages, were Christians and charitable. One of them did not
permit me to depart till it appeared that I should be well able to reach
the village I was bound for. In it I met with more than seventy
Spaniards. The chief [O'Rourke] was not there. He had gone to

defend a territory which the English were coming to take; and although a savage, he is a very good Christian and an enemy to heretics, always carrying on war with them. Early next day about twenty of us Spaniards collected together at the house of Señor de Ruerque in order that they might give us something to eat, for the love of God; and while we were there begging, news was told us that a Spanish ship was at the coast, that she was very large and came for those Spaniards who had escaped. With this news without waiting longer, the whole twenty of us left for the direction where they told us the ship was, and we met with many hindrances on the way, though for me it was an advantage and a mercy which God granted me that I did not arrive at the port where she was in the same manner as the others. They embarked on board of her, as she belonged to the Armada, and had arrived there in a great gale with her mast and rigging much injured. They set sail from thence in two days with the crew that came in her and those that they had picked up, only to run aground and get wrecked on the same coast. More than two hundred were drowned, and those who reached the shore by swimming were taken by the English and all put to the sword. I alone remained of those that went in search of her. Going along thus, lost, with much uncertainty and toil, I met by chance a clergyman in secular clothing (for the priests go about thus in that kingdom, so that the English may not recognise them). He was sorry for me, and spoke to me in Latin, asking me to what nation I belonged and about the ship′wrecks that had taken place. God gave me grace so that I was able to reply to everything he asked me in the same Latin tongue; and so satisfied was he with me that he gave me to eat of that which he had with him, and he directed me by the right road that I should go to reach a castle [Rossclogher] which was six leagues from there. It was very strong, and belonged to a savage gentleman [MacClancy], a very brave soldier and a great enemy of the Queen of England, and of her affairs, a man who had never cared to obey her or pay tribute, attending only to his castle and mountains, which made it strong.

They helped me as best they could with a blanket to wear of the kind they use and I remained there three months, acting as a real savage like themselves. The wife of the chieftain was beautiful in the extreme, and showed me much kindness. One day we were sitting in the sun with some of her female friends and relatives, and they asked me about Spanish matters and other parts, and in the end it came to be suggested that I should examine their hands and tell them their fortunes. Giving thanks to God that it had not gone even worse with me than to be gipsy among the savages, I began to look at the hands of each and to say to them a hundred thousand absurdi- ties which pleased them so much that there was no other Spaniard better than I or that was in greater favour with them.

The custom of these savages is to live as brute beasts among the mountains which are very rugged in that part of Ireland where we lost ourselves. They live in huts made with peat. The men are large bodied and of handsome features and limbs; and as active as the roe-deer. They do not eat oftener than once a day and this is at night; and what they usually eat is butter with oaten bread. They drink sour milk, for they have no other drinks; they do not drink water although it is the best in the world. On feast days they eat some flesh half- cooked without bread or salt. They clothe themselves in light trousers and short loose coats of very coarse goat's hair. They cover themselves with blankets and wear their hair down to their eyes. They are great walkers and inured to toil. They carry on perpetual war with the English, who keep garrison for the Queen. The chief inclination of these people is to be robbers, and to plunder each other; so that no day passes without a call to arms among them. The most of the women are very beautiful, but badly dressed. They do not wear more than a chemise and a blanket, with which they cover themselves and a linen cloth, much doubled over the head and tied in front. They are great workers and housekeepers, after their fashion. These people call themselves Christians. Mass is said among them, and regulated according to the orders of the Church of Rome. The great majority of their churches, monasteries and hermitages have been demolished by the hands of the English and of those natives who have joined them and are as bad as they. In short, in this kingdom there is neither justice nor right, and everyone does what he pleases.

These savages liked us well because they knew we came against the heretics and were such great enemies of theirs, and if it had not been for those who guarded us as their own persons, not one of us would have been left alive. We had goodwill to them for this, although they were the first to rob us and strip to the skin those who came alive to land; from whom and from the thirteen ships of our Armada, in which came so many people of importance, all of whom were drowned, these savages obtained much riches in jewellery and money.

Words of this reached the great Governor of the Queen, who was in the city of Dublin and he went immediately with 1,700 soldiers to search for the lost ships and the people who had escaped. They were not much fewer than a thousand men, who without arms and naked, were wandering about the country in the locality where each ship had been lost. The majority of these the Governor caught, and hanged them at once or inflicted other penalties, and the people who he knew had sheltered them he put in prison and did them all the injury he could. In this manner he took three or four savage chiefs who had castles, in which they had sheltered some Spaniards; and, having put both parties under arrest, marched with them along the whole of the coasts till he arrived at the place where I was wrecked. From thence he turned off towards the castle of Manglana [MacClancy], for so they called the savage with whom I was, who was always a great enemy of the queen and never loved anything of hers, nor cared to obey her, for which reason he (the Governor) was very anxious to take him prisoner. This savage, taking into consideration the great force that was coming against him, and that he could not resist it, decided to fly to the mountains, which was his only remedy: more he could not do. We Spaniards who were with him had news of the misfortune that was coming upon us, and we did not know what to do, or where to place ourselves in safety. One Sunday, after Mass, the chief with dishevelled hair down to his eyes, took us apart, and, burning with rage, said that he could not remain, and had decided to fly with all his villagers, their cattle and their families, and that we should settle what we wished to do to save our lives. I replied to him to calm himself a little, and that presently we would give him an answer. I went apart with the eight Spaniards who were with me – they were good fellows – and I told them they should well consider all our past misfortunes and that which was coming upon us, and in order not to see ourselves in more, it was better to make an end of it at once honourably. We should not wait any longer, nor wander about, flying to the mountains and woods, naked and barefoot, with such great cold as there was. Besides, as the savage regretted so much abandoning his castle, we, the nine Spaniards who were there, would cheerfully remain in it and defend it to the death. This we could do very well, even if there should come two other forces more than the

one that was coming, because the castle is very strong and very
difficult to take even if they attack with artillery for it is founded in a
lake of very deep water, [Lough Melvin], which is more than a
league wide at some parts, and three or four leagues long and has an
outlet to the sea; and besides, with the rise of spring tides it is not
possible to enter it, for which reason the castle could not be taken by
water nor by the shore of the land that is nearest to it. Neither could
injury be done it, because for a league round the town, which is
established on the mainland, it is marshy, breast deep so that even
the natives cannot get to it except by paths. Considering all this
carefully, we decided to say to the savage that we wished to hold the
castle and defend it to the death; that he should, with much speed,
lay in provisions for six months and some arms.

The chief was so pleased with this, and to see our courage, that he
did not delay much to make all provisions, with the goodwill of the
principal men of his town, who were all satisfied. And, to ensure
that we did not act falsely, he made us swear that we would not
abandon his castle nor surrender it to the enemy for any bargain or
agreement, even if we should perish from hunger; and not to open
the gates for Irishman, Spaniard or anyone else till his return, which
he would doubtless accomplish. Then with all that was necessary
being well prepared, we moved into the castle, with the ornaments
and requisites for the Church service and some relics which were
there, and we placed three or four boat loads of stones within [as
missiles] and six muskets and six crossbows and other arms. Then
the chief, embracing us, returned to the mountains, all his people
having gone there already; and the report was spread throughout the
country that Manglana's Castle was put in a state of defence, and
would not be surrendered to the enemy because a Spanish captain,
with other Spaniards who were within, guarded it. Our courage
seemed good to the whole country, and the enemy very indignant at
it, and came to the castle with his forces – about 1,800 men – and
observed us from a distance of a mile and a half from it, without
being able to approach closer on account of the water which inter-
vened. From thence he exhibited some warnings and hanged two
Spaniards and did other damages to put us in fear. He demanded
many times by a trumpeter that we should surrender the castle, and
he would spare our lives and give us a pass to Spain. We said to him
that he should come closer to the castle, as we did not understand

him, appearing always to make little of his threats and promises. We had been besieged for seventeen days when our Lord saw fit to succour and deliver us from that enemy by severe storms and great falls of snow, which took place to such an extent that he was compelled to depart with his force and to march back to Dublin, and from thence he sent us warning that we should keep ourselves out of his hands and not come within his power, and that he would return in good time to that country. When he [MacClancy] got news that the Englishmen had retired, he returned to his town and castle greatly appeased and calmed, and they fêted us much, the chief offering whatever was his for our service, and the chief persons of the country [did the same]. To me he offered to give a sister of his in marriage. I thanked him much for this but contented myself with a guide to direct me to a place where I could meet with a ship for Scotland. He did not wish to give me permission [to leave], nor to any Spaniard of those who were with him, saying that the roads were not safe; but his sole object was to detain us, that we might act as his guard.

So much friendship did not appear good to me, and so I decided, secretly, with four of the soldiers who were in my company to depart one morning two hours before dawn so that they should not pursue us on the road; and also because one day previously a boy of Manglana's had told me his father had said that he would not let us leave his castle till the King of Spain should send soldiers to that country; and that he wished to put me in prison so that I might not go. Possessed of this information, I dressed myself as best I could and took to the road with the four soldiers, one morning ten days after Christmas. I travelled by the mountains and desolate places enduring much hardship and at the end of twenty days' journey I got to the place where Alonzo de Leyva and the Conde de Paredes and Don Tomás de Granvela were lost [the Giant's Causeway, Antrim], with many other gentlemen, to give an account of whom would need a quire of paper, I went to the huts of some savages there who told me of the great misfortunes of our people who were drowned at that place and showed me many jewels and valuables of theirs which distressed me greatly.

My chief cause of misery was that I had no means of embarking for the kingdom of Scotland; until one day I heard of the territory of a savage whom they called Prince Ocan, where there were some vessels that were going to Scotland. Thither I travelled, crawling along, for I could scarcely move because of a wound in one leg; but, as it led to safety, I did all I could to walk and reach it quickly. The vessels had left two days before, which was no small disappointment for me, as I was in a very dreadful country and among enemies, there being many English stationed at the port, and each day they were with Ocan. I did not know what to do, as the soldiers who came with me had left and gone to another port further on to seek for a passage. Some women when they saw me alone and ill, pitied me, and took me away to their little huts on the mountain and kept me there for more than a month and a half in safety and cured me, so that my wound healed, and I felt well enough to go to Ocan's village to speak with him, but he did not wish to hear or see me. The English who were quartered there having marched to invade a territory, Ocan had accompanied them with all his force, so that one could go openly about the village, which was composed of thatched huts. In them were some very beautiful girls, with whom I became very friendly, going into their houses occasionally for society and conversation. One afternoon, while I was there two young Englishmen came in, one who was a sergeant and possessed of information of me, by name, but yet had not seen me before. When they were seated, they asked me whether I was a Spaniard, and what I was doing there. I said Yes, I was one of the soldiers of Don Alonzo de Lucon who had lately surrendered to them, but on account of a bad leg, I had not been able to leave the district; that I was at their service to do whatever they wished to command. They told me to wait a little, and that I should have to go with them to the city of Dublin, where there were many important Spaniards in prison. I said I could not walk or go with them and so they sent to search for a horse to carry me. I told them I was very willing to do whatever they wished, and to go with them, with which they were reassured, and began to make fun with the girls. Their mother made signs to me to get out, and I did so in great haste leaping banks as I went along. I got among thick brambles into which I penetrated until I lost sight of Ocan's castle, following this course until I wished to lie down for the night. I had arrived at a very large lake on the banks of which I saw a herd of cows and two boy savages. I spent two days with them, being treated with much kindness. One of the boys had to go to the village of the Prince of Ocan to ascertain what news or rumour there was, and he saw the two Englishmen going about, raging, in search of me. The boy was such a good lad that, upon learning this, he returned to his hut and informed me, so I had to leave very early in the morning and go in search of a bishop who was seven leagues off in a castle where the English kept him in banishment and retirement. This bishop was a very good Christian and went about in the garb of a savage for concealment, and I assure you I could not restrain tears when I approached him to kiss his hand. He had twelve Spaniards with him for the purpose of passing them over to Scotland, and he was much delighted all the more so when the soldiers told him I was a captain. He treated me with every courtesy that he could for the six days I was with him, and gave orders that a boat should come to take us over to Scotland, which is usually done in two days. He gave us provisions for the voyage and said Mass to us in the castle, and spoke with me about some things concerning the loss of the kingdom and how his Majesty had assisted them; and that he would come to Spain as soon as possible after my arrival in Scotland, where he advised me to live with much patience, as in general they were all Lutherans and very few Catholics. The bishop was called Don Reimundo Termi, an honourable and just man. God keep him in His hands and preserve him from his enemies. That same day at dawn I went to sea in a wretched boat with eighteen persons and, the wind being contrary, we were forced to run before it, at the mercy of God, for Shetland, where we reached land at daylight, the boat being nearly swamped and the mainsail carried away. We went on shore to give thanks to God for the mercies He had bestowed on us in bringing us there alive; and from thence in two days with good weather, we left for Scotland, where we arrived in three days; not without danger on account of the great quantity of water the miserable boat took in.

It was said that the King of Scotland protected all the Spaniards who reached his kingdom, clothed them and gave them passage to Spain, but all was the reverse, for he did no good to anyone, nor did he bestow one real in charity. Those of us who reached that kingdom suffered the greatest privations. I am inclined to believe that he was much persuaded by the Queen of England to hand us over to her, and, had not the Catholic lords and counts of that kingdom helped us – and there were many, and great gentlemen to favour us and speak for us to the King, without doubt we should have been betrayed and handed over to the English. For the King of Scotland is nobody; nor does he possess the authority or position of a king: and he does not move a step nor eat a mouthful that is not by order of the Queen. Thus there are great dissensions among the gentlemen, who bear him no goodwill and desire to see his reign ended and the majesty of the King our master in his place, that he might establish the Church of God which has been brought to such ruin there. This they said to us many times, almost weeping, longing to see that day which they hoped in God might soon arrive.

There was a Scotch merchant in Flanders who offered and agreed with his Highness [the Duke of Parma] that he would come to Scotland for us and ship us in four vessels with the provisions which were necessary and that he would bring us to Flanders, his Highness giving him five ducats for each Spaniard.

All was treacherous; for an agreement had been made with the ships of Holland and Zeeland that they should put to sea and await us at the entrance to the harbour of Dunkirk, and there put us all to death, without sparing one. The Dutch did as they were commanded and were on the look⁄out for us for a month and a half. God willed that of the four vessels in which we came two escaped and grounded, where they went to pieces; and the enemy, seeing the means of safety which we were taking, gave us a good discharge of artillery. They could not come to our assistance with the boats from the port of Dunkirk, as the enemy cannonaded them briskly. On the other hand, the sea and wind were very high so that we were in the greatest peril of being all lost. However we cast ourselves afloat on timbers, and some soldiers were drowned, as was also a Scotch captain. I reached the shore in my shirt without any other clothing. It was sad to see us enter the town once more, stripped naked, and for the other part we saw before our eyes, the Dutch making a thousand pieces of 270 Spaniards who came in the ship which brought us to Dunkirk, not leaving more than three alive; for which they are now being paid out, as more than 400 Dutchmen who have been taken since then have been beheaded.

From the city of Antwerp,

                                        Francisco de Cuellar

Launch of Fireships